Plaster Effects   112
   Polished Venetian Plaster   114
   Multicolored Venetian Plaster   116
   Stenciled Venetian Plaster   118
   Embossed Textures   121
   Lace Designs   123
   Plaster with Mix-ins   124
Special Effects   126
   Clouds   128
   Wood Graining   130
   Spattering   132
   Frottage   134
   Tissue Paper Texture   136
   Marbling   139
Metallic Effects   142
   Brushed Metal   146
   Hammered Metal   148
   Metallic Pot   150
   Gold Leaf   154
Choosing Colors for Metallic Effects   158
Antique Effects   160
   China Crackle   162
   Aged Crackle   164
Lime Paint and Lime Wash   166
   Lime Paint   168
   Lime Wash   171

PREPARING TO PAINT   172
Patching Holes   174
Smoothing Out a Textured Wall   178
The Importance of Primer   180
Painting Surfaces Other Than Walls   182

RESOURCE GUIDE   188

CREDITS   189

INDEX   190

COLOR
transformations

IT MAY BE A CLICHÉ to say that nothing transforms a room as quickly or as economically as paint. But there's a reason this point is so often made: It's true. Fresh paint covers dirty fingerprints, masks wear and tear, and makes a space look fresh and clean. Add color and even more magic happens. What was once a hectic area may suddenly seem calm and restful, or a sterile room can come to life. The power of color to transform space is that strong.

Faux and decorative techniques allow you to fine-tune plain paint to give your rooms just the look you want. These changes can be subtle, with translucent color layered over a similar shade of opaque paint, or bold and brassy thanks to new metallic paints.

This chapter shows how some clever people have used decorative paint in their homes. It also walks you through the process of selecting colors, materials, and tools, and then getting the paint expertly onto your walls. With these basics, you'll be ready to tackle the projects that follow. Chapter 3 guides you through issues you will face if your walls need repair or if you are painting surfaces other than walls.

▶ Decorative paint techniques can be tailored to virtually any décor, from ornate Victorian styles to contemporary settings. This modern living room features mottled paint as a colorful background to Le Corbusier furniture.

decorative PAINT
& FAUX FINISHES

By Jeanne Huber and the Editors of Sunset Books
Menlo Park, California

Sunset Books

V.P., GENERAL MANAGER: Richard A. Smeby
V.P., EDITORIAL DIRECTOR: Bob Doyle
PRODUCTION DIRECTOR: Lory Day
DIRECTOR OF OPERATIONS: Rosann Sutherland
MARKETING MANAGER: Linda Barker
ART DIRECTOR: Vasken Guiragossian
SPECIAL SALES: Brad Moses

Staff for This Book

MANAGING EDITOR: Bridget Biscotti Bradley
WRITER: Jeanne Huber
ART DIRECTOR: Amy Gonzalez
PRINCIPAL PHOTOGRAPHER: Chuck Kuhn
COPY EDITOR: John Edmonds
PROOFREADER: Meagan C. B. Henderson
INDEXER: Nanette Cardon
PRODUCTION SPECIALIST: Linda M. Bouchard
PREPRESS COORDINATOR: Eligio Hernandez

ISBN-13: 978-0-376-01389-7
ISBN-10: 0-376-01389-3
Library of Congress Control
Number: 2006923295
Printed in the United States of America.

For additional copies of *Decorative Paint & Faux
Finishes* or any other Sunset book, visit us at
www.sunsetbooks.com or call 1-800-526-5111.

COVER: Photography: Jamie Hadley
Photo Styling: JoAnn Masaoka Van Atta
Decorative Painting: Karen Talbott/Pigments
of Imagination
Paint Technique: Venetian plaster
Design: Vasken Guiragossian

This book would not have been possible without the help of many fine painting professionals,
especially Patricia Rushon of Refined Finishes,
as well as Bruce Carter and David P. Schott of
Interiors Only, color consulant Mary Jane Rehm,
and the staff of Winslow Paint Company.
Thanks also to painters Jesse Arter of Ochres &
Oxides, Natthamon Wutilertcharoenwong, and
Elijah Distefano.

CONTENTS

COLOR TRANSFORMATIONS   4
The World of Decorative Painting   6
Choosing a Color Scheme   18
Types of Decorative Paint   26
Choosing Texture Materials   34
Choosing the Right Painting Tool   36
Techniques to Ensure a Great Paint Job   42
Cleaning Up After a Paint Project   50

CREATING DECORATIVE EFFECTS   52
Deciding on a Project   54
Mottled Looks   56
    Mottling with a Rag   58
    Mottling with Cheesecloth   60
    Mottling with a Brush   62
    Mottling with a Two-part Roller   63
    Mottling with a Feather Duster   64
    Mottling by Rag Rolling   65
Choosing Colors for Mottled Looks   66
Geometric Designs: Blocks, Stripes, and Diamonds   68
    Moiré Stripes   72
    Limestone Blocks   75
    Dry-brushed Blocks   78
    Diamonds   80
Choosing Colors for Geometric Designs   84
Dragged Effects   86
    Strié   88
    Linen   90
    Small-scale Combed Designs   92
    Combed Checks   94
    Plaid   97
    Rolled Squares   98
Choosing Colors for Dragged Effects   100
Stencils   102
    Stenciled Border   106
    Raised Stencil   109

THE WORLD
of decorative painting

Fabulous walls don't have to cost a fortune. Today, virtually all paint companies offer the materials that allow you to wash your walls with translucent color or add texture or pattern to plain surfaces. Light, bright, animated, subdued, aged—whatever mood you want for a room, you can use paint and decorative techniques to help create it.

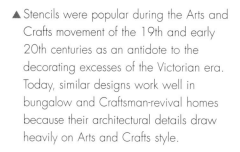

▲ Stencils were popular during the Arts and Crafts movement of the 19th and early 20th centuries as an antidote to the decorating excesses of the Victorian era. Today, similar designs work well in bungalow and Craftsman-revival homes because their architectural details draw heavily on Arts and Crafts style.

▶ All-over painted stencil designs on this stairway wall creates the look of wallpaper. Using metallic paint for both the base color and the stenciled areas results in a particularly striking look. The base color is Platinum and the stenciled areas are Tequila Gold, both colors in the Modern Masters line of metallic paints.

◄ Polished venetian plaster looks textured, but it feels silky smooth. Today, venetian plaster is available in acrylic formulas that are relatively easy to apply, as well as in the trickier original mixture of lime putty and marble dust.

▼ Mottling, which combines two or more colors that swirl around and over each other, is one of the most common decorative techniques. The random design of the mottled paint on the wall sets off the plant stand.

◄ Narrow stripes make walls seem higher, a useful trick in rooms with low ceilings. If you have walls that are very high, you can still indulge in stripes without making the walls seem out of scale. Visually shorten the stripes by embellishing the top and the bottom of the wall with stencils or blocks or both, as was done here.

formal spaces

Decorative paint yields large rewards in formal rooms. Without changing expensive features such as molding, furniture, or carpeting, you can dress up the room or make it seem more relaxed. Glazing the walls with translucent color warms large spaces, for example. It also makes them seem more intimate. Flashier techniques, such as stenciling or gilding, emphasize décor based on historical themes.

▲ A special paint technique often adds just the right amount of decoration to a formal room that's kept free of fussy details. This long, narrow dining room features a chandelier and architectural details that include leaded-glass doors and wainscoting, but the walls are adorned only with mottled paint.

◀ Subtly mottled paint on the walls conveys the impression of old-fashioned stucco, which fits the stylistic mood of this living room.

▶ Just as flowers owe their showy look partly to the relatively drab green foliage in the background, jazzy furnishings stand out against muted colors. Here, the white trim and mottled gray walls bring out the drama of a red heart-shaped seating arrangement.

▲ Hand-polished venetian plaster and sunny yellow paint on the woodwork give this living room a refined gleam. Light bounces off shiny surfaces and brings spaces like this to life.

▲ Metallic paint or sheets of imitation gold leaf make a room's trim sparkle. To stop short of overpowering glitz, consider gilding only parts of the trim, as the painter of this room did. Like jewelry with a simple black dress, a little gilding often looks more elegant than a lot.

9

casual spaces

In informal rooms, you can use decorative paint as a stand-in for more expensive ornamental details, such as wallpaper or elaborate molding. You can also use paint to personalize the space and to establish a tone for the activities you want to encourage there. Where you want quiet, restful activities, for example, you can color-wash the walls with a subdued tone. Where you want people to gather for laughter and play, shift the colors in the opposite direction.

▼ A top-of-the-wall stenciled design mimics elaborate crown molding in a room where the actual molding is narrow and plain. The simple stencil and the mottled walls create a fitting backdrop for the colonial-style furniture.

▲ Khaki-colored lime paint provides subtle tone variations on these living room walls and accentuates the exposed-beam ceiling.

▶ Glazed with a grayish purple, mottled walls serve as a soft background for strong accent pieces. To create a texture similar to this, dab the glaze with a rag that has been arranged so its folds leave an imprint.

◄ Horizontal stripes may look labor intensive, but a clever approach makes them easy. Tightly wrapping masking tape around the middle 3 inches of a 9-inch-long roller leaves the 3 inches on each end elevated. Like circular rubber stamps, these areas pick up and deposit paint to create the stripes. Here, the wall was first painted an ivory color, then the stripes were rolled on.

▼ Mottled paint adds interest to tall walls in an informal living room. The bright color, along with the abundance of windows, creates a cheerful space that invites people to gather here.

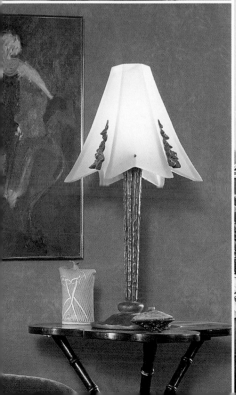

small-scale impact

Powder rooms, bathrooms, and other small spaces often warrant special attention when it comes to paint. After all, where else do people have as much time to contemplate your handiwork? In a small room, elaborate paint treatments don't become overwhelming, as the room's size automatically limits the effect. Plus, in a small space, you can indulge in techniques that might be too time consuming on a larger scale.

▲ Trompe l'oeil, or "fool the eye," paintings typically require an artist's touch, but even those with little training can tackle simple designs that depend mostly on geometric shapes. For a stone column similar to this, for example, you could use the stone block technique shown on page 75. You could mottle the main expanse of wall, as shown on pages 58–59, then add the vine either by painting it freehand or by stenciling it in. Adding a mirror doubles the effect with no work on your part, and it adds the illusion of space to a small room.

▶ Hand-painted or stenciled designs add whimsy to a bathroom wall. A pattern of simple, repeating images is more subdued than a mural-style painting or stenciled design. Painting accents in the same color as the room's trim also keeps the overall effect from seeming gaudy.

▼ Where rooms have beautiful tile, you can use decorative paint to extend the effect higher on the walls. In this bathroom, the tile design reappears, in paint, as a demure crown molding. Mottled paint softens the walls and ceiling.

▶ An intriguing collection of small stencils, linked by a theme only you know, gives visitors something to think about when they visit your little room.

▲You can also combine decorative paint techniques to create the look of fresco. First use a mottling technique to paint the main expanse of wall, then add hand-painted or stenciled accents. Finish up by antiquing the surface with sandpaper or a tea-colored glaze.

floors and ceilings

When people think about painting a room, most of their attention goes to the walls, then perhaps to the trim. The ceiling and floor may not get a second thought. But these large surfaces have a tremendous impact on the overall look of the space. You can transform them with decorative paint techniques just as readily as you can the walls. However, if you have fairly low ceilings, go easy on overhead decoration. It can make the ceiling seem even lower than it actually is.

▲ Wispy clouds create a heavenly feel. In this bedroom, the ceiling is further accentuated because the walls are draped.

◄ A painted diamond pattern on the wood floor makes a narrow galley kitchen seem wider than it is.

▶ Stenciled designs work well on floors. For a subtle effect, use pale colors that pick up tones used elsewhere in the room.

▲ A delicate stenciled design and blocks of slightly contrasting color make an overly high ceiling seem lower. The colors are muted and light, giving the room an airy feeling.

▲ Paint transformed this once-dark attic into a spare bedroom. Instead of replacing the floorboards, the owners simply painted them. Besides adding welcome color, the plaid design helps counteract the strong linear look of the boards.

children's rooms

In children's rooms, you can indulge in paint effects that might seem too flashy or sentimental elsewhere. Children love personal touches, and you can use paint to spark their creativity and support their play activities. Clouds and stenciled designs are common, but you can also experiment with blackboard paint, glow-in-the-dark paint, and even metallic paint. Don't worry about coming up with a decorating theme that will carry on through the years. As children grow older, they develop ideas of their own and will probably want to paint over whatever you come up with initially.

▲ Brilliant color establishes this room as a child's realm. Wall decorations like this can be done freehand or with stencils. For the striped table, you could adapt the wall stripe technique shown on pages 72–74.

▶ Children love enclosed spaces that can easily metamorphose into playhouses or forts. An alcove bed serves splendidly. The doors and drawer fronts also make an ideal canvas for special paint techniques, such as stenciling. Lettering like this can be painted freehand or stenciled.

◄ In their early years, children often spend considerable time in that dreamlike state between wake and sleep. Cloud scenes, stenciled designs, and other decorative paint techniques encourage creative thought and can serve as backdrops to stories you tell.

▶ Simple geometric designs work well in a child's room, especially if you combine them in slightly unusual ways. Here the diamond painted floor runs at a 45-degree angle to the striped walls. This twist adds a touch of animation, as do the creatures on the bedspread and pillows.

CHOOSING
a color scheme

Whether you plan to paint a single room or a whole house, the first step may prompt you to stall. Given that there are thousands of paint colors, how do you select the right ones for your project?

▲ Look for color inspiration in everyday things, like this collection of bright sap buckets whose colors pop off a darker grayish purple wall.

◄ A color can appear dramatically different depending on how light bounces off the surface, as the ceiling in this room shows.

Luckily there are more helpful resources than ever. Begin by paging through this book. Pick out a room or project you like and then match the colors, or select a combination from pages 66–67, 84–85, 100–101, or 158–159. You can also look through magazines and tear out photographs. See page 20 on using a color wheel, which can help you select good combinations.

Color combinations generally look best when they have similar white, black, or gray tones. For example, if you use a light blue, use a light yellow or gold rather than a bright yellow. If you pick a bold color to dominate a room, bright colors will work best as accents.

Here are some other issues to consider:

APPARENT TEMPERATURE Green and blue are cool colors, while yellow, red, and orange are warm. People actually feel more or less comfortable because of them. Use cool colors to overcome an oppressive feeling in a west-facing room on a summer afternoon, or warm colors to make a cold north-facing room seem cozier. Most rooms use combinations of both cool and warm colors. Choose which to make dominant by the effect you want to create.

PSYCHOLOGICAL MOOD A dark entry that opens to a light living area makes the main room seem brighter and more inviting. Pastel tones, especially with green or blue as a base, make a room seem subdued and serene. Yellow and orange are lively colors. Red and purple are warm and intense, particularly effective in dining areas that you use at night. And what if all you want is white? It has color too. You can warm up a cold room by choosing white paint that has a bit of red or yellow mixed in, or cool down a hot room with white that has a green or blue tint. The tints are often so pale that you notice them only when two whites are next to each other. Take advantage of this if you want to emphasize moldings. Paint them a contrasting white.

PRACTICAL EFFECTS Dark colors absorb light waves rather than bounce them back, so if you paint too many surfaces dark colors, you will have to provide more artificial lighting at night if you want to see well. Yellows and yellow-based colors brighten dark areas. Gray-based colors tone down overly bright rooms.

ROOM SIZE Dark colors make rooms seem smaller, while light colors make them seem larger. To visually raise a ceiling, extend the wall color to the top of the wall or even onto the ceiling and paint any crown molding the same color. To lower a ceiling, continue its color down partway onto the walls. Add emphasis with molding that separates the colors, or stencil in a horizontal design that goes around the room at or above the height of the top trim on doorways.

▼ In a room where the walls merge into a low ceiling, mottled paint preserves the color-reflecting quality of light paint but still hints at the cozy effect of dark paint on walls and ceilings.

checking your colors

NO ONE CAN LOOK AT A PAINT CHIP that covers one or two square inches and be sure of having selected the best color. Look for oversized paint chips that some manufacturers now offer, or purchase sample-size jars or packets of paint. Test paint on drywall scraps or pieces of foam core (sold at stationary stores) or hardboard rather than on your walls. This way you can check the color in different parts of a room and see how different light conditions and adjacent surfaces affect the color. Paint the test boards with primer first so the sheen and color are the same as what you will get on your walls. See page 41 for tips on how to test decorative effects.

using a color wheel

As children, most of us learned some basic color theory. We smeared yellow and blue paint together and came up with green. Or we mixed yellow and red and saw orange. By adding white, we turned colors into pastels. With black, we made bright colors dark. In the end, most wound up looking like mud because we mixed too many colors together. Those lessons are the basis of the color wheel, a tool that helps predict which shades look good next to each other and how their combinations influence the mood of a room.

A color wheel shows the effects of combining equal amounts of two primary colors (yellow, red, or blue) to make a secondary color (orange, purple, or green). It also shows the results of blending a primary color and a secondary color to make a tertiary color, such as yellow-green or blue-purple. The wheel shows how pure color is altered with the addition of white, which in color lingo makes a tint; black, which makes a shade; or the opposite (or complementary) color, which produces a grayish tone. Using the wheel, you can pick many successful combinations.

MONOCHROMATIC For a quiet, restful look, stay on one spoke of the wheel to get a single color adjusted with different amounts of white, black, or gray.

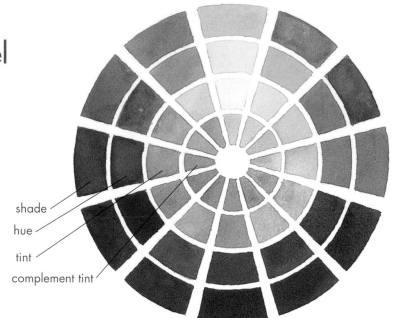

shade
hue
tint
complement tint

ANALOGOUS To add a bit more life to a room but keep its overall effect quiet, select three colors side by side, each with similar amounts of white, black, or the complementary color. You might pick one color for most of the room and use the others as accents on accessories.

COMPLEMENTARY For the liveliest look, choose two colors opposite each other on the wheel: red and green, blue and orange, or purple and yellow. You don't need to stick to pure colors. Consider those with equal amounts of white, black, or gray.

SPLIT COMPLEMENTARY If you like unusual combinations, select one color plus those on each side of its complement. Again, use similar intensities.

DOUBLE-SPLIT COMPLEMENTARY For something even more intriguing, use four colors—the ones on either side of a pair of complementary colors. You can also select three shades that are an equal distance apart on the color wheel. Unless you want primary colors as your theme, select shades that have been similarly toned down with white, black, or gray.

▼ You can often use color combinations from the natural environment to select paint colors. This living room gets its color scheme from both the upholstery fabric and the bird of paradise flowers.

A quilt can inspire paint colors. This room manages to be both cheery and calm because of the two key colors, rose and sage green. Basically, these colors are red and green. As complementary colors, opposite each other on the color wheel, they produce the most vivid, energetic look. However, the rose and sage green used here are shifted slightly from true red and green, and each has a little of the other color mixed in. This makes the colors more gray, muting their contrast. Using the green as the dominant color also adds to the calm feeling in the room.

The striking paint colors on this stairway follow the color theme of the rug at the base of the steps. For a match like this, it works best to shop for the rug first because paint is available in virtually any color.

shortcuts to good color combinations

If you're in a quandary about how to select the best color combination, consider piggybacking on the artistic decisions that went into a piece of fabric or an illustration that you like. Simply pick out the individual colors that were used and then decide which parts to execute in paint and which to carry out with fabric, flooring, or other elements.

This approach works best if you are starting from scratch or want to redecorate completely. It's perfect, for example, if you recently purchased a new house and are confronted with room after room of white or off-white.

If you are working with existing furniture and flooring that you don't want to change, start with colors in the upholstery or carpet.

Be sure to factor in the color of any woodwork that you don't want to change, especially the color of a wood floor, which may be the most dominant surface in the room.

tip FOR EXPERT ADVICE, find a good color consultant. Ask someone at your local paint store for recommendations. You may be able to arrange a short, free consultation at the store. Expect to pay perhaps $100 per hour for a visit to your home, where the consultant can check light levels and factor in your furnishings. An hour-long consultation may be all you need, and it could save you from repeatedly testing paint or winding up with colors you don't like.

making rooms flow together

Some houses are filled with a jumble of decorating styles, while others have décor that's pulled together and organized. The difference often stems from color choices. Though most people redecorate one room at a time, the way the colors relate from one room to the next is important. To create a harmonious look, you have several options.

SELECT ONE COLOR THEME Use it throughout the house, but play up the colors in different ways. In one room, you can use a specific color as the dominant hue. In an adjoining room, that color might show up only in accessories.

▲ The three primary colors—yellow, red, and blue—all play prominent roles in the main room of this house. With that as a starting point, the white woodwork would unify almost any color combination in the rest of the house as long as the colors are bright rather than pastel or gray.

▲ Decorative paint techniques, as well as the colors in them, affect whether you will have a smooth or an abrupt transition between rooms. One concept that works is to stick with the same technique on surfaces that you see together, even if the colors are different.

REPEAT ONE COLOR If you want different color schemes, repeat one color in each room. Make the unifying color dominant in one room and use it for accessories, trim, or other supporting roles elsewhere.

MAKE GRAY THE UNIFIER Use different color schemes, but select colors that are similar in intensity or grayness in each room.

USE CONSISTENT TRIM Unify different color schemes in various rooms by painting baseboards, molding, doors, and windows one color. If you plan to paint built-in woodwork, consider sticking with the same color for it as well.

BRIDGE WITH BEIGE If you want a different color scheme in every room, paint hallways or transition alcoves beige or another neutral color.

▲ Just as complementary colors within a room help energize a space, complementary colors used from one room to the next make it fun to move through a house. Here the designer selected colors close together on the color wheel for the walls in adjoining rooms but used aqua and green, the complementary colors of those hues, as accents.

◄ A window in a nearby sidewall illuminated every imperfection in this living room's end wall, so the homeowner decided to celebrate the wall's imperfections and make them more obvious by applying a cross-hatched pattern with plaster. Framed by a neutral-colored plaster, the rich yellow plaster seems almost like a canvas on a museum wall.

where to use decorative paint

Though it's possible to indulge in decorative paint techniques through-out a house, it often makes more sense to create special effects where they will have the most impact.

An accent wall makes a great canvas. But to work well, the surface must really be worthy of playing that star role. Consider the following places for your masterpiece.

FRAME WALLS Decorative paint techniques are especially helpful on walls that frame the view from one room to the next. If you use colors found in both rooms, you can tie the spaces together.

ALCOVES AND ARCHES If your house has interesting architectural features, play them up with decorative paint. Ceiling features, such as arches and vaulted shapes, deserve special attention.

FIREPLACE SURROUNDS When fireplaces were built of stone or brick and burned wood, they needed to be massive to absorb and store heat. Now that many fireplaces burn only natural gas or propane, some are so slimmed down that they have little visual impact. With decorative paint, you can put the emphasis back on a feature that still resonates as the emotional center of a home.

▶ In expensive kitchens, elaborate tile designs often accentuate the stove as the center of kitchen activity. You can create a similar effect with paint.

▼ Coated with polished venetian plaster, a curved wall embraces a modern vanity and creates a setting that seems almost like a piece of functional art.

decorative paint made portable

SOME DECORATIVE PAINT techniques are quick and easy. If you move or change your mind and decide to repaint, the time and money you invested in creating the painted surface is no great loss. But it's also possible to create special effects in such a way that you can easily move them and restore the original look of the walls. If you're a renter with a landlord not fond of experimentation, this may be a good approach, especially for techniques that alter the texture on the walls. For example, you can hire an artist to paint a focal point in a room where you have used an easy decorative technique, such as mottling. To make the focal point portable, have it painted on ⅛-inch-thick hardboard or on canvas. For added interest, have the painting set at an angle, as shown below.

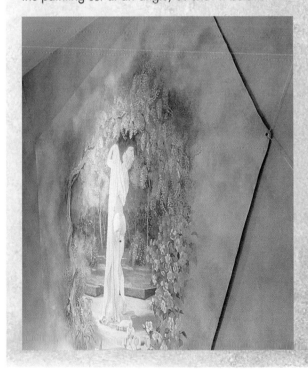

INTIMATE SPACES In homes where most ceilings are quite high, people seem to linger in areas where ceilings are low and cozy. You can emphasize these gathering spots with decorative paint, or even create a similar cozy feeling with decorative paint in areas with high ceilings. Dark ceilings, especially with glossy paint, or ceilings that have patterns or other decorations seem considerably lower than ones that are flat white.

▲ Accents aren't only for showy spaces. In a laundry area, you can create an accent wall that will bring a smile to your face as you sort and fold.

TYPES OF
decorative paint

To create the finishes shown in this book, you will need basic painting materials and tools, plus a few specialty items. Luckily, the exploding interest in faux and decorative paint means these supplies are increasingly easy to find at paint stores and home improvement centers, not just through specialty companies.

UNDERSTANDING PAINT

Whether you stick with standard paint or opt for the techniques shown later in this book, you will of course need paint. It helps to understand a bit about what goes into every can. There are three main components: pigment, which provides the color; solvent, which makes the paint easy to spread but then evaporates so you're left with a dry film; and resin, also called binder, which is the glue that holds the ingredients together and sticks them to the wall or other surface.

Old-fashioned paint typically included mineral spirits, also known as paint thinner, as the solvent. The traditional binder was linseed oil, pressed from flaxseeds, although alkyd, a synthetic, eventually became much more common. Traditional oil paints cured because the linseed oil or alkyd combined with oxygen once on the wall. The resulting chemical reaction produced a tough plastic-like film.

▲ Glossy paint has long been used for trim, and it also makes the best base for decorative paint techniques. Because glossy paint contains more resin than flat paint, it has a slicker surface. On trim, that's important because fingerprints wipe off more easily. As a base for decorative paint, the smooth surface allows you to move glaze layers where you want them.

Today, most paint used in houses has water as its main solvent. The resin is often acrylic, or vinyl, or a combination of those plastics. Though water-based paint is often referred to as latex paint, the resin is never true latex, the milky sap of rubber trees. Like oil-based paints, water-based finishes cure into a tough film, but getting it to form correctly is trickier than it is with oil-based paint. The water has to evaporate at just the right rate so that the little bits of plastic resin in the paint can merge properly.

All of the techniques detailed in this book were accomplished with water-based materials. Oil paint and glaze do, however, work well. Some painters prefer them because oil paints don't dry as fast. They are also easier to sand.

HOW DECORATIVE FINISHES DIFFER

To paint walls and trim, most people want fast-drying paint that covers everything in one coat, doesn't drip, and dries to a fairly thin film that

the surface evenly porous. Without primer, some areas are likely to absorb more paint than others, which causes a wall to look splotchy. You probably won't notice it as you paint, only after the paint dries. The problem may persist even after several coats of finish paint. It's a lot less frustrating, and less work and expense, to do the right preparation from the beginning.

A few decorative finishes go right on top of primer. But in most cases, you must top the primer with two coats of base paint and wait for them to dry thoroughly before you proceed. Select an eggshell or semigloss sheen for the base so the surface will be slick enough for you to manipulate a glaze layer. Flat paint is too rough, though you'd need a microscope to see the texture. The roughness is what makes the paint nonreflective.

doesn't mask details of molding or other surface decoration. As a result, most house paint is formulated to meet these standards. It dries to the touch quickly, though the underlying paint usually remains soft and even slightly tacky for several weeks.

When you embark on decorative painting, however, you often need paint that dries more slowly so you have time to move it around on the wall. You may need it thicker than usual so you can create textured effects. And you might want a translucent wash of color, not an opaque paint. The special ingredients used in decorative painting fulfill these demands.

▲ Though dark walls add drama, too much can be overpowering. White wall panels and trim are a good antidote. Because the framed Asian print of a horse also uses bright white as a background, the room's color scheme focuses attention on the artwork.

PREPARATION All techniques shown in this book assume you are beginning with a properly prepared wall or other surface. That means you need to fill any cracks, holes, or depressions and then paint the wall with a primer-sealer (see pages 174–181). This type of paint grips well to materials such as drywall and patching compounds, and it makes

▲ A brilliant orange glaze over yellow paint energizes this small bathroom.

mixing and using glazes

Most faux and decorative paint techniques depend on the use of glaze, a translucent finish that stays fluid long enough for you to move it around on a wall. Water-based glaze contains acrylic resin, just as water-based paint does, plus extenders that delay drying and ingredients that control drips and other factors.

Glaze is sometimes called paint without the pigment. When wet, it looks milky white. It dries clear unless you add color. The type of colorant determines which kind of glaze you should buy. If you want to tint the glaze with paint, buy classic glaze. If you or the paint store will tint it with universal colorants (the same pigments used to tint paint), buy scumble glaze, also known as tintable glaze. Check the glaze label to make sure you use the correct colorant.

DETERMINING QUANTITIES When you use standard paint, you can check the label to determine how many square feet a container will cover. With glaze, however, the coverage depends on the technique you plan to use.

■ If you will coat the entire surface with glaze and then wipe some of it off, figure that a gallon of tinted glaze will go about as far as a gallon of paint, typically 400 square feet. Simply adjust the coverage according to the formula you are using for tinting the paint. For example, if you mix 1 quart of paint and 3 quarts of glaze, you can cover approximately 400 square feet.

■ If you will apply the glaze formula only to patches of the wall and then rub the color out into adjoining areas, the glaze mixture will go much further. One gallon might cover 500 to 600 square feet or more.

■ To calculate the square footage for a project, multiply the length or height times the width of each surface you will paint, then add the results. For a more precise figure, subtract the space of any doorways, windows, or other areas that will not require paint.

KEEPING GLAZES WET In hot, dry weather, glaze may dry faster than you can manipulate it. Minimize problems by working on a cool, humid day, preferably in the morning. Turn off overhead fans and the air-conditioning or heating system. If this isn't enough, add an extender to lengthen the wet or "open" time of the glaze, or increase the proportion

▲ Glazes make paint translucent and movable, so it's possible to blend and overlap colors in a way that resembles what artists accomplish with watercolor.

of glaze if you are using the type of glaze that's tinted with paint.

MIXING GLAZES When you mix classic glaze and paint, the color becomes significantly lighter. But water-based glazes darken as they dry. Always create a test sample (see page 41) to be sure you have the color you want.

For a subtle effect, select a paint chip color that you envision for the overall effect. Then test it using base paint that's one shade lighter and glaze that's two shades darker. When mixing glaze and paint, always measure accurately so you can replicate the results. Most recipes call for "parts" of paint and glaze, which means you can use a base measurement appropriate to your project. For test samples, that might mean a tablespoon or two of paint and a multiple of that amount for glaze. For a larger project, you might measure by the cup or quart.

Use the recipes at right as a guide, but always test before you embark on your project. The opaque glaze, because it contains relatively little base, will dry very fast. You may need to add an extender if you use it for a large project.

If the glaze seems sticky rather than slippery as you move it around to create the look you want, increase the proportion of glaze. If that results in too light a color, get a darker paint to mix with the glaze.

tip WHERE A GLAZED SURFACE is likely to collect dirty fingerprints or food splatters, add a protective coating, such as flat or satin acrylic, shellac, or another clear finish. Otherwise, repeated cleaning will wear off some of the glaze.

basic glaze recipes

OPAQUE GLAZE

1 part latex paint

2 parts glaze

This recipe is appropriate for dragged finishes, such as strié (see pages 88–89). It has a shorter open time than mixtures with a higher concentration of glaze, so be sure not to apply it to too large an area at once.

MEDIUM GLAZE

1 part latex paint

4 parts glaze

This is the basic formula, one that will work for almost any technique. It's especially suitable where you want to create mottled looks (see pages 58–65) or blend several colors together, such as in the stone project on pages 75–77.

TRANSLUCENT GLAZE

1 part latex paint

8 parts glaze

When you want to "tea stain" or "antique" a surface, this translucent glaze is ideal. You can also use it to create very subtle mottled looks.

mixing your own colors

To create custom colors for glazes, you can incorporate dry pigments, artist's acrylics, or universal colorants, the basic pigments that paint companies use to formulate hundreds of colors. Besides supporting creative urges, this approach allows you to buy a single container of glaze and then use it to create several colors. Because you tint only as much as you need, you're less likely to wind up with numerous containers of partially used material.

There are some caveats, however. Keep excellent notes so you can replicate colors. Even so, be aware that new batches might not match. The smaller the quantity of colorant in your recipe, the harder it is to measure exactly. Also, because you will likely use products from various companies, there's no way to be certain they are all compatible. Be sure to prepare test samples.

POWDERED PIGMENTS Old-fashioned paint got its color primarily from finely ground clay or chalk that was rich in iron oxides and trace minerals. Some paint stores still carry these pigments, along with ones created from heated colored earth or whose chemistry was replicated in a factory. At a home center, you may find

POWDERED PIGMENTS

a limited selection near bagged concrete mixes, since earth pigments are also used to tint concrete. The pigment may be sold as powder or dispersed in water.

If you are using dry pigment, wear a disposable respirator so you don't inhale the dust while you measure and mix. Stir the pigment and a little water into a paste, then add more water to make a free-flowing liquid. Stir that into water-based paint or glaze. Using a thick paintbrush as a stir stick helps break up clumps of dry pigment, but you may still wind up with tiny beads that burst while you are painting, causing streaks of color. Powdered pigments are ideal

LIQUID ARTIST'S ACRYLICS

PASTE ARTIST'S ACRYLICS

for tinting lime paint (see pages 166–171) for just this reason. They enhance the handmade, old-time plaster look of this type of finish.

ARTIST'S ACRYLICS
Sold as densely colored paste in tubes or as liquid in small jars, these are perfect for projects that cover small areas, especially where you want vivid colors. Standard house paint is formulated so that stores can create hundreds of colors merely by tinting base paint with specific amounts of perhaps 16 pigments. Though there are separate base paints for pastels and deep colors, the formulas aren't optimized for the specific shade you select. With artist's acrylics, however, each color is manufactured with the exact pigment that's needed. This results in more intense, vivid color.

Besides using artist's acrylics straight from the tube or bottle, you can use them to tint water-based paint or the type of glaze that can be mixed with paint. Mix paste acrylics with a little water before you incorporate them into paint or glaze. You don't need to add water if you are using liquid acrylics.

▼ One advantage of mixing your own colors is that you can stir up small batches to paint small areas or to create stenciled designs. This greatly reduces the quantity of leftovers.

UNIVERSAL COLORANTS Some paint stores sell universal colorants—the basic pigments that companies use to formulate hundreds of colors—by the bottle or tube. Besides buying the pure colorants that go into the paint-mixing machine, you may find mixtures that correspond to specific colors on paint chips. Some paint companies don't sell universal colorant but may give it to you if you buy glaze and supply a tight-sealing container for the colorant. If you get enough colorant to tint a quart of paint, you'll likely have plenty to make glaze for your project. Colorants go approximately ten times further in glaze than they do in paint.

▲ When you need small amounts of vivid color, such as for the medallion on this wall, consider using artist's acrylics rather than standard wall paint. The colors are more intense because the formula is optimized for the specific color.

These are the universal colorants needed to tint a quart of paint or perhaps a gallon of glaze to the purple color shown, called Mask. The formula calls for relatively large amounts of white, black, and magenta, plus a dot of blue.

premixed specialty paints

For most decorative effects, all you need is glaze plus standard house paint or universal colorants. But there is also a rich array of premixed specialty paints that you may want to incorporate into your designs.

BLACKBOARD An entire wall can become a message or art center when you use blackboard paint. For best results, apply it to a smooth, hard surface, such as hardboard, not to textured drywall. Cover the surface with primer and two coats of blackboard paint. Allow it to dry for as long as the manufacturer specifies, often three days, before anyone draws on it.

▲ While this wall looks aged and handmade, the effect was actually created with a roller and the Sand Finish product in Benjamin Moore's Studio Finishes Latex Texture line. Despite the product's name, it contains no actual sand, which would tend to settle at the bottom of the can. The manufacturer uses a material that stays suspended better.

TEXTURED Textured paint adds interest to a wall and hides minor surface defects. The material is thick and not tinted. Apply it with a wide, hefty brush or with a damp roller. When the texture dries, coat it with paint and possibly glaze.

GLOW IN THE DARK With glow-in-the-dark paint, you can create designs that appear to be either milky white or translucent while a room is lit but glow when the room

▶ Glow-in-the-dark paint from Benjamin Moore makes that last evening trip to the bathroom a lot more fun.

▲ Not just for the school room, blackboard paint invites doodlers to take a break from computer work at home.

darkens. Standard glow-in-the-dark paint uses zinc sulfide as its phosphorescent agent. A five-minute charge equips the paint to glow with a greenish-white color for about 20 minutes. This paint is the type you are most likely to find in paint stores.

From specialty companies, you can buy paint and glow-in-the-dark powder that produces more light for longer periods and in different colors. Some are translucent, so you may want to use a black light as you paint if you want to see what you're creating. Glow-in-the-dark designs work best over white or other light-colored backgrounds.

SUEDE Suede paints create a velvety texture thanks to tiny particles, often plastic beads, that are suspended in the formula. The texture resembles 220-grit sandpaper, but it's softer. Generally, you apply the first coat with a roller and allow it to dry. For the second coat, you use a wide paintbrush and make a series of overlapping X's. This simulates the random texture of natural suede. If you were to just roll, you'd see lines where your passes overlapped.

LIME WASH Lime wash adds a chalky white glaze and a slight texture to your walls. Designed to mimic the effect you'd get by painting plastered walls with true lime paint or whitewash, the material is pasty and thick, though not as thick as most other textured coatings. Apply lime wash with a big brush, as if you were a friend of Tom Sawyer's working on that fence.

METALLIC Some metallic paints mimic real metal quite well. Because

▲ Dead flat but softly textured, the Suede Impressions finish from Valspar helps set a calm mood in a home office.

they contain a considerable amount of actual metallic powder, they even tarnish over time like many metals do. You can speed up the process by coating this type of paint with a patina solution. Other metallic paints are available in vivid colors, including blue, purple, and orange. Though these may include small amounts of recycled metal, their sheen comes mostly from mica. These paints don't develop a patina.

▶ Using metallic paint for both a base coat and a stenciled design creates a finish that resembles ornate wallpaper. Here, the base paint is Ivy, and the stencil design is Warm Silver, both from Modern Masters.

CHOOSING
texture materials

Although you can paint flat designs that appear to be three-dimensional, many decorative effects look far more realistic when they're created with materials that have actual texture. Decorative painters use an array of materials to create raised designs and textures that resemble rustic plaster, stone, and brick.

ALL-PURPOSE DRYWALL MUD

Also known as drying-type joint compound, this is the standard material for covering nail or screw holes and seams between sheets of drywall. Though you can purchase it as a powder, premixed paste is easier to use. Drywall mud is inexpensive, readily available, easy to manipulate, and relatively soft. This makes it easy to sand. It's also easy to dent, so for decorative effects, use drywall mud on surfaces that are looked at but not bumped against.

Drywall mud shrinks as it dries, and it dries relatively slowly—maybe in 24 hours, depending on how thickly you apply it. Speed up the process by turning on a heater. If you texture a surface with drywall mud and don't like the effect, you can usually just scrape it off, provided you haven't covered it with paint or glaze. After that, as with other texture materials, you have to either sand it off or cover it with a smooth layer of drywall mud.

SETTING-TYPE DRYWALL MUD

Also known as hot mud or quick-setting joint compound, this material sets because of a chemical reaction that starts when you add water to the powdered product. Specific products have different setting times, ranging from 5 minutes to 3½ hours. You can speed up the setting by using hot water, but you can't

▶ This textured wall was skim-coated with drywall mud and then painted.

▼ Venetian plaster develops a slightly mottled look when it is rubbed with a trowel after it dries. Areas that are a bit elevated darken because they become polished more than areas that are slightly depressed.

slow it down, so prepare only as much as you can use within the allotted time.

Most setting-type compounds dry so hard that they are difficult to sand or scrape off. A few are softer and sandable. Setting-type compounds shrink very little as they harden.

GESSO Found at arts and crafts supply stores more than at paint stores, gesso is a liquid material that you can apply in layers to create texture. Although gesso was traditionally made from fine chalk and size, or animal glue, most products today have an acrylic base.

VENETIAN PLASTER Traditional venetian plaster, used since the Middle Ages, consists primarily of aged lime putty and marble dust. It's a beautiful finish but generally best left to pros to create. Paint stores sell acrylic blends that mimic the look of the original formula and are easier to apply. Venetian plaster is tougher than drywall mud, so it's a better choice in rooms that get heavy use. Also, unlike both types of drywall mud, venetian plaster is easy to tint. Use universal colorants to tint acrylic-type venetian plaster, and universal or powdered earth pigments for traditional types. Or mix with artist's acrylics or water-based paint, provided a thinner consistency will work for your technique.

FAUX TEXTURE PASTE Companies that specialize in faux and decorative paint produce a variety of texture materials. Some products are formulated to remain porous so they work well with glazes.

DRYWALL MUD

GESSO

VENETIAN PLASTER

FAUX TEXTURE PASTE

CHOOSING THE RIGHT
painting tool

Most decorative paint techniques begin with two base coats of standard paint, often over a coat of primer. For these initial coats, you need only standard painting tools. Brushes, rollers, and foam pads all can be useful, but each works best for a specific purpose.

BRUSHES When you need to cut in at the edges of a room or paint trim, brushes deliver paint most precisely and efficiently. Common advice is to buy the best brush you can afford. That's true when you want to get a lot of paint onto a surface and wind up with a smooth finish. But for touch-ups and some decorative techniques, inexpensive brushes work better because they hold less paint and are therefore easier to clean.

Flagged ends minimize brush marks.

Long, thick bristles hold lots of paint.

Pair of hardwood spacers creates mini reservoirs for paint.

Thick resin block holds bristles securely.

Rust-free ferrule won't discolor paint.

Hefty hardwood handle is easy to hold for long periods.

This brush has synthetic bristles, suitable for all types of paint.

Rustproof nails hold ferrule securely to handle.

HIGH-QUALITY BRUSH

Short bristles with flagged ends hold less paint (ideal in certain circumstances). This version has natural bristles, which can swell when exposed to water-based paint and glaze.

Rust-prone ferrule is no problem unless brush is damp for long periods.

Staples hold ferrule to handle.

Thin resin block allows brush to shed bristles.

INEXPENSIVE "CHIP" BRUSH

Single wooden spacer

Thin softwood handle

In general, choose brushes with synthetic bristles for use with water-based paint, as natural bristles swell when damp. However, inexpensive "chip" brushes, which have natural bristles, can be used with water-based paints and glazes in some decorative techniques for which this tendency to swell doesn't matter.

■ For cutting in, a 2-inch-wide brush works well.

■ For painting thin trim, such as window muntins, use a 1½-inch-wide angled brush, which keeps paint in a thin line.

■ If you want to get a lot of paint onto a surface fast, use a brush with long, thick bristles. For a smooth finish, get a brush with bristles that are fuzzy on the ends. Look for bristles trimmed into a chisel tip, not cut off flat.

■ Chip brushes, which have short, thin bristles, are ideal when you want to keep the brush as dry as possible, such as when you are creating a strié finish (see pages 88–89) or metallic color blocks (see pages 78–79).

ROLLERS To paint a wall or a ceiling quickly and evenly, use a roller. There are two and sometimes three parts: the metal frame, which you can easily reuse indefinitely; the cover, which you can reuse or replace

before each job; and an optional extension handle that can help eliminate trips up and down a ladder.

■ Rollers come in a wide array of widths and diameters. Small, thin "weenie" rollers are great for painting both sides of a corner at once and for applying finish to small areas, as you may do often if you create decorative effects. Big, wide rollers are most efficient for painting large areas.

■ Match the nap (or pile) length to the texture of the surface you are painting. On smooth walls, use a short nap. On rough surfaces, such as heavily textured walls or masonry, use a longer nap.

■ Use roller covers made of synthetic materials such as nylon or polyester with water-based paints and glazes. Mohair and lamb's-wool rollers are for oil-based finishes only.

■ If you want the option of using extension handles, buy a frame

FOAM PADS

ROLLER COVERS IN DIFFERENT SIZES

with a handle that has threads on the end. Use a long handle for ceilings; it saves you from working on a ladder except when you are cutting in edges. For walls, you may find that a medium-length handle, 2 or 3 feet long, is less awkward.

FOAM PADS Foam pads are great for touch-ups, and some people prefer them for painting even large wall expanses because the paint goes on evenly, without any of the spattering that can occur when you use a roller. If you do use a pad to paint a large area, scrape excess paint from the pad occasionally so it doesn't drip.

For touch-ups or painting small areas, use pads about an inch wide. They're designed for use on a bent handle, which makes painting hard-to-reach areas a breeze. For covering large walls, use wide pads. Thin pads are suitable for flat walls, while thicker pads work better on textured surfaces.

tools used for decorative effects

You can accomplish many decorative techniques with only basic painting tools. But numerous specialty tools, often quite beautiful, are also available. They make certain techniques easier, or they enable you to create more subtle effects than you might otherwise be able to pull off.

DUAL ROLLER, RAG ROLLER, SPONGE ROLLER

CHEESECLOTH AND RAGS

To remove and manipulate glaze and to blend colors, you can use either cheesecloth or rags. Cheesecloth has a finer texture, but rags are more readily available and are often free.

The best cheesecloth has a close, even weave, and can be bought by the yard. Cheesecloth sold in little packages at hardware and grocery stores tends to have thinner fibers and a looser weave. It's less absorbent and may be scratchy enough to mar fresh paint.

The best rags are made from old cotton T-shirts torn or cut into fairly large pieces. You can make them or buy them by the box or bag. Professionals always use white

SEA WOOL SPONGE

rags to make sure no dye transfers to the wall. Pure cotton is more absorbent than cotton-polyester blends.

SPONGES Natural sponges are great tools for applying and removing paint and glaze. Left behind by millions of minute creatures once clustered on the ocean floor, a sponge is essentially a bunch of storage

vessels. Each has numerous inlet valves and one big outlet. This allows the sponge to sop up a liquid from one surface and deposit it onto another. For example, you can use a sponge to pick up paint from a tray and get it onto a wall without any drips. The sponge's natural, slightly irregular texture also makes a pleasing pattern.

Get the type of sponge known as sea wool. Select a nicely rounded piece that's soft even when dry.

SPECIALTY ROLLERS Designed to make decorative painting easier and quicker, these allow you to create special effects that are ordinarily done by hand. Dual rollers get two colors of paint on the wall at once.

SPECIALTY BRUSHES Though you can apply most decorative finishes with standard brushes and rollers, special brushes can help create certain effects.

Inexpensive chip brushes are good for removing excess paint and for blending glaze colors. Because the bristles are short and sparse, chip brushes are easy to wipe or rinse

T-SHIRT RAG   HIGH-QUALITY CHEESECLOTH

STENCIL BRUSHES

CHIP
BRUSHES

OVERGRAINER

STIPPLERS

GRAINING
ROCKER

clean, a big help when you're creating a strié effect (see pages 88–89) or a linen look (see pages 90–91). The bristles become limp when exposed to water, but this just helps them blend glaze colors more subtly.

Stipplers have stiff bristles tightly packed together, allowing you to "pounce" or poke at the paint to distribute it across a surface. Most stipplers are quite large, like scrub brushes, and have hog or horse hair. Stencil brushes are similar but smaller.

Blending brushes have very soft badger bristles. Use them to blend colors or to create subtle moiré patterns in strié designs. Don't dip these brushes into finish; just use them to lightly blend paint or glaze already on the wall. Rinse the bristles frequently, shake off excess water, and blot them on a cloth before you resume work.

Artist's brushes are great for touch-ups and accent details, and they help get paint into tight spaces. Have one small brush with a flat tip so you can paint or touch up a thin line, one small brush with a pointed tip for when you need just a dot of touch-up paint, and one larger brush with a pointed tip, which you can use to fill in larger areas.

Graining tools, available in numerous styles, help create faux wood and

marble effects. Pull rockers through glaze as you rock the tool back and forth to make a wood grain or moiré pattern. Overgrainers have bristle bundles that each act as a small brush. Use them to produce parallel wood grain lines. Slap floggers sideways into wet glaze so the long horsehair bristles create openings that look like wood pores.

FLOGGER

BLENDING
BRUSHES

ARTIST BRUSHES

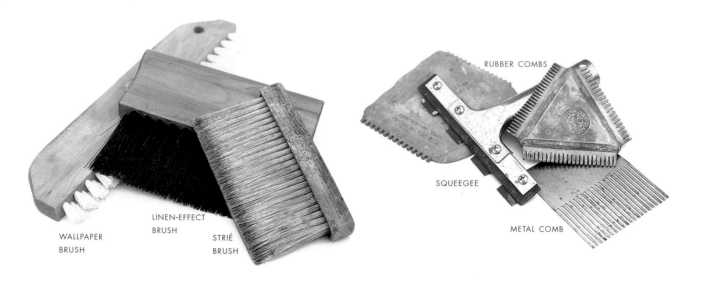

WALLPAPER BRUSH

LINEN-EFFECT BRUSH

STRIÉ BRUSH

RUBBER COMBS

SQUEEGEE

METAL COMB

COMBS AND DRAGGING BRUSHES

These toothed tools and sturdy brushes create rows of parallel lines by removing fresh glaze wherever the teeth or bristles touch the wall. Some combs are triangular, with teeth of a different width on each side. You can also make your own custom-sized comb by cutting teeth into the rubber blade on a squeegee. Manufacturers sell special dragging brushes to create strié and fabric looks, but other brushes also work.

SPATULAS AND TROWELS

These tools are used to apply venetian plaster and other texture materials. Professionals often use steel or stainless-steel spats that have a wooden handle along one edge of the blade. To apply venetian plaster, they often use stainless-steel masonry trowels, sold at stores that specialize in concrete and plaster supplies. If you can't find or afford the specialty tools, you can improvise with an inexpensive drywall knife. Get one with a wide, flexible blade and round the corners with sandpaper (see page 115). To get texture material into tight spots, you can always cut off the drywall knife's handle so the tool mimics a true spat.

SPATULAS

DRYWALL KNIFE

a straight trowel

TROWELS USED TO APPLY and polish venetian plaster must be flat and flexible. Those used to apply drywall mud look similar but won't work. Their edges dig into the surface and scratch it. Also, many drywall trowels aren't actually flat. Their blades bow slightly to leave a small hump of joint compound over seams.

VENETIAN PLASTER TROWEL

DRYWALL TROWEL

practicing on sample boards

Creating the decorative techniques shown in this book requires practice. Do this on sample boards, not your walls. Make the boards from foam core, hardboard, or drywall scraps, and paint them with the same primer and base that you will have on your walls. If you are using foam core or hardboard, prime both sides to keep them from curling and to double your practice area.

Though you should allow paint and glaze on walls to dry naturally, you can speed up the process for sample boards by setting them in the sun or using a hair dryer on them. Too high a heat, however, may alter the colors slightly. Rapid drying might also cause texture materials to crack.

■ If you are working out color combinations, you might be tempted to add dabs of various colors to get just the shade you want. This is fine. But to get a batch of paint or glaze large enough to coat a room, you will need to replicate the color. Save a little of each color in a small jar and label it. Color changes as a finish dries, so a wet sample is easier to use as a reference to match.

■ If you are preparing numerous sample boards, attach them to hangers with clothespins so you can set them out to dry without using up all the horizontal surfaces in your workspace.

TESTING CORNERS Corners present special problems with many decorative paint techniques because you're likely to smudge the finish if you paint both walls at once. There are two solutions:

■ Paint one wall and wipe smudges off the adjoining wall. Let the finish dry before you paint the second wall so you can safely wipe its smudges off the initial surface.

■ Apply painter's tape to one wall. Paint the other wall. Remove the tape and clean off any excess finish that pooled along the tape edges. Wait for the finish to dry, then repeat for the other wall.

With either approach, apply finish a few inches away and use a chip brush to dab some of it into the corner so you don't get too much there. Practice first on sample boards made of drywall or foam core. Use painter's tape to secure the boards to a corner of a room while you conduct your tests.

▶ To make a sample board with a corner, use foam core or drywall. First score a line on the back with a utility knife.

▼ Flip the board over and bend the sides inward to form the corner.

TECHNIQUES TO ENSURE
a great paint job

You're lucky if you are embarking on a paint project simply because you don't like the existing color. When the walls, ceiling, and trim are already painted and are still in basically good shape, you face the most streamlined painting job possible, especially if you leave the ceiling and trim as they are and paint only the walls. But you could still wind up with a mess if you just slap on the paint.

For a sparkling new finish that's smooth and even, with no drips and no thin areas where you can see through to the old paint, use the time-tested procedures adopted by top-notch professional painters. Always apply two coats of finish paint, not just one. You can stop there or go on to embellish the finish with the decorative techniques shown in this book.

If your walls are in rougher shape, you have some work to do before you paint. Beginning on page 172 you'll find resources for dealing with more complex situations, such as heavily textured walls or holes that must be patched. In that section, you'll also find tips on painting ceilings, doors, and windows.

SETUP Before you open your first can of paint, take the time to organize your work area. In the garage or on a large piece of cardboard or scrap plywood, set out all the tools and materials you'll need, including those for cleaning up afterward. Provide a garbage can or bag so you have a place to put painter's tape that you peel off while paint drops on it are still wet.

REMOVE GRIME Paint won't stick to dirt and oily fingerprints. Even if your walls look like they're ready for paint, give them the white-glove test. With a clean white cotton cloth, dust the walls and look for areas that need washing. If the cloth picks up grime, wash the entire surface and allow it to dry before you proceed. Always wash kitchen and bathroom surfaces so you're sure to remove food spatters and soapy splashes. Use water with a few drops of detergent or with a TSP-type cleaner, then rinse well.

CLEAR AND COVER Move furniture out of the room or push heavy pieces toward the center and cover them with a drop cloth. Spread other drop

▲ Though paint can seep through a canvas drop cloth, it rarely does. To keep partially dried drips from coming off onto the surface you are trying to protect, always place the cloth so that the same side is up. Pack the cloth with the painted face folded in on itself. This way, the back may show paint stains but won't have clumps of paint.

cloths over the floor. Each type has advantages and disadvantages.

■ Plastic drop cloths block spills but are slippery, and thin plastic can tear. These cloths are best for covering furniture in the center of the room.

■ Pros generally use canvas, which is durable and not slippery. Though paint can seep through the fabric, canvas is thick enough that small spills dry on the surface. For even better protection, some pros use rubber-backed canvas.

■ Brown paper drop cloths with a plastic layer in the middle are impervious and not slippery. They're better than plastic on the floor but not as durable as canvas.

basic tools and materials

- Drop cloths
- Stepladder
- Paintbrush to use as a mini broom
- Low-tack painter's tape and paper tape
- Synthetic brush for cutting in along corners
- Bucket for paint
- Roller frame and two covers (one for primer, one for top coats)
- Paint tray that fits roller
- Stir stick
- Paint key or flat screwdriver to open paint cans
- Painter's 5-in-1 tool
- Drywall knife (with flexible blade)
- Clean white rags
- Plastic bags to cover tools and paint trays between steps
- Bucket of wash water
- Disposable plastic gloves
- Respirator that filters out latex paint fumes
- Garbage can or bag

tip IF THE WALLS ARE CLEAN and don't need patching, you may be able to skip the primer, and possibly even the base coats if the color is right and the paint is relatively glossy. If it's flat, coat the wall first with glaze. If in doubt, glaze or paint.

◄ You must work quickly once painting begins, so plan a way to keep key tools close at hand. One solution, shown at left, is to use belt or pant loops and pockets to carry a damp cotton rag, a brush to use as a mini broom, and a 5-in-1 tool (see below). You can also strap on a bucket filled with a couple of inches of paint to use when cutting in.

ONE HANDY TOOL

Although it's called a 5-in-1, this enhanced drywall knife does even more tasks.

Point cleans out cracks so you can patch them.

Sharp edge scrapes off dried paint, removes small bulges; also works as a chisel tip.

Blunt edge opens paint cans and works in a pinch as a flat screwdriver.

Curved scraper removes dried paint from rounded edges.

Teardrop works as a nail puller; the tip catches even small-head nails.

Curve scrapes excess paint from rollers.

Handle acts as a hammer to tap down nails or lids of paint cans.

masking surfaces you don't want to paint

With a steady hand and a lot of experience, professionals learn to paint right up to molding or a corner without masking the adjoining surface. But for peace of mind and neater results, it's usually better to cover adjoining surfaces before you begin painting.

Smoothing tape along a surface seems simple enough, but aspects of the job can be frustrating. If you find a rounded corner, for example, it's unclear where the tape should go. Or you may pull off tape at the end of a job and find that paint seeped underneath and left a ragged edge. Using the following tips will help ensure good results.

WORK IN SEQUENCE If you are painting adjoining surfaces different colors, you don't need to mask between them until you get to the second color. But make sure not to leave drips of paint behind on the surface you will paint next, as big blobs remain visible even after you paint over them.

■ If you are painting all surfaces in a room, paint the ceiling first. Then mask the ceiling and paint the walls. Finally, mask wall surfaces next to trim and paint the trim.

■ If you are painting only the walls, mask the ceiling and the trim from the beginning.

■ Though you should start at the top and work down when you paint,

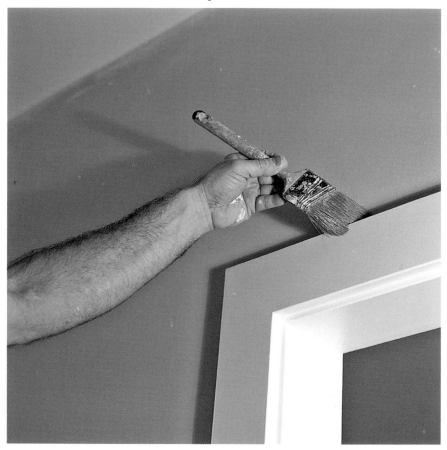

▲ Use a small paintbrush to sweep surfaces before you apply tape.

attach masking materials in the opposite order, beginning with the floor, so that layers overlap in a way that doesn't allow any drips to run behind the masking.

DUST FIRST Dust inevitably collects on the top of doorway trim and other horizontal surfaces such as baseboards. Brush off these surfaces before you apply painter's tape or it won't adhere properly. If the debris doesn't brush off, the surface is probably oily. Wash it off and let the surface dry before you apply tape.

APPLYING TAPE Avoid stretching tape when you apply it. Unroll a workable length or cut a piece long enough for the section you want to mask. Working in short stretches, align the edge that will establish the paint line, then gently press the tape down and smooth out any wrinkles. Repeat for the next section. When you're done with an area, go over the tape again to seal the edges to the surface.

◀ Keep the tape slightly away from the rounded corner so you can establish a straight paint line.

▼ Immediately after applying each coat of wall paint, remove the painter's tape (but not the paper) so you can clean off any paint that seeped underneath. For the second coat, just put down fresh painter's tape since the paper tape is already in place.

MASKING BASEBOARDS Where a wall meets the baseboard, a bead of caulk often creates a rounded, irregular corner. It's a difficult spot to tape because there's no clear place where the wall paint should stop and the trim color should begin. Place the tape so that it is completely on one surface or the other.

Instead of depending on painter's tape to protect the baseboard from spatters, use the tape in combination with paper (brown for water-based paint, green for oil paint). Place the paper first so it's about half an inch away from the edge of the wall, then cover the gap with painter's tape.

◀ When you're taping off trim in a corner, use separate pieces of tape in each direction. Extend the first piece all the way into the corner. Cut off the next piece at a 45-degree angle, as if it were a mitered picture frame. To cut the tape neatly, tear it along a sharp edge, such as the front of a painter's 5-in-1 tool or a drywall knife.

Because the corner joining a wall and a ceiling is rarely perfect, you'll wind up with a crooked line if you attempt to align the tape exactly in the bend. Instead, place the tape just beyond the corner, on the ceiling. People won't notice whether the ceiling and wall colors meet right in the corner, but they will see whether you painted in a straight line.

PREVENT SEEPAGE Few things are more frustrating than taking the time to carefully tape off all corners and molding, only to discover later that paint seeped underneath. Carefully pressing down the tape helps, but it's not foolproof. Try painting over the tape with the color you are trying to protect before applying the new color. Paint may still sneak under the tape. But after you paint the wall and remove the tape, the seepage will match the ceiling and you'll see a straight line. If you don't have left-over ceiling paint, brush on the wall paint from the tape edge out so that you don't push paint under the tape.

PROTECTING THE CEILING To keep wall paint from getting onto the ceiling, you need to mask its outside edge. One challenge is what to do with the roll of tape when you need one hand to align the tape and the other hand to press it into place. The solution is to first cut the tape to the approximate length you need. If you then drape the tape across the room, you'll have both hands free to position it exactly where you want it.

▲ Extend the tape across the room and tear off the approximate length you need, plus a few inches. Temporarily stick one end to the wall near a corner. Starting at the other end, you can then climb a ladder and use both hands to position the tape.

▶ To keep wall paint from seeping under the tape and marring the ceiling, brush some of the ceiling paint along the edge of the tape.

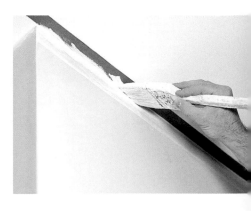

REMOVING TAPE Though painter's tape isn't supposed to pull off paint that's underneath, it still sometimes does. Minimize problems by removing the tape at a moderate rate. If you yank it off too fast, the tape may tear off in slivers. If you pull too slowly, you increase the chance of removing the paint underneath. Start by pulling the tape at a 45-degree angle to the surface. If that leaves adhesive residue behind, slow down and widen the angle so that you are pulling the tape at 90 degrees relative to the wall.

2-INCH PAINTER'S TAPE

1-INCH PAINTER'S TAPE

masking tapes

MASKING TAPE used to be available only in tan, but today you can buy blue, green, white, and gray. Each color is a code signaling how well the tape adheres and which finishes it might damage. Unfortunately, what the colors mean differs from one manufacturer to the next, so you can't use them as a guide without reading labels or checking store displays. If you're unsure, ask a clerk to make sure you buy tape that suits your needs.

CREPE PAPER TAPE The original tan masking tape, this relatively high-tack material works well where you are covering curves or bumpy surfaces. Remove it promptly, especially in direct sun, or it is likely to leave a stubborn residue.

PAINTER'S TAPE This is smoother tape, generally medium-tack, though low- and high-tack types are also available. For most painting projects, use medium-tack tape and remove it within the number of days that the manufacturer recommends. However, if you are creating a decorative finish and find that medium-tack tape doesn't stay in place over a glazed surface, switch to a higher-tack product. Be sure to test it first and remove it promptly.

FINE-LINE TAPE Stores typically sell masking tape as narrow as ½ inch, but for decorative paint projects such as stone blocks (see pages 75–77), you may need tape that's even narrower. If your paint store doesn't have it, ask at an auto body shop for fine-line tape, which detailers use when they paint stripes on cars.

¼-INCH MASKING TAPE

PAPER TAPE

applying the paint

When you've finished masking surfaces that won't be painted, return your attention to the walls. Inspect them carefully for little imperfections that are easy to fix now but difficult to deal with later.

FINAL FIXES Shine a bright light against the walls at an angle to reveal little dents, such as those made when someone bumped furniture into the wall. A dab of lightweight spackle quickly dispatches these flaws, as well as holes left by nails that once hung pictures. See pages 176–177 for tips on patching large areas.

AT LAST, THE PAINT You are now ready to begin painting. But first make sure you have the time you will need. Water-based paint dries quickly once it goes on a wall, and junctions between dried paint and wet paint will show. Don't rush the painting, but don't dawdle either.

Before you begin painting, dampen your brush with water (assuming you are using water-based paint) and then shake out the excess. This helps keep paint from drying on the brush and makes it easier to clean afterward. Dip bristles into the paint no more than one-third of the way. Avoid wiping the brush against the rim of your bucket or can to remove excess

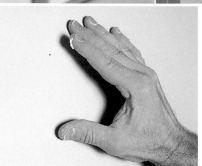

▲ Feather out the edges of the paint you cut in so that you don't leave a thick ridge, which will show through the rolled-on coat.

◄ When you fill a nail hole with light-weight spackle, you can paint over it immediately.

paint, as doing so leaves the brush too dry. Instead, tap the loaded brush against the sides of the container a couple of times.

CUTTING IN Begin painting by coating the edges of the wall, a process known as cutting in. Use a brush or a paint pad, not a roller, so you can apply the paint more precisely. Though you may be tempted to cut in around every corner or piece of molding so that you can then roll on the paint without interruption, if you cut in only one wall and then finish that wall before you move on to the next, the paint around the edges should still be damp enough that you won't see a line between sections.

FILLING IN To paint the main expanse of the wall, use a roller. Moisten the roller with water (assuming you are using water-based paint) and spin out the excess. This preconditioning improves the roller's performance and makes it easier to clean at the end of the job. Stir the paint well, then pour some into the bottom well of the tray, being careful not to overfill it. Run the roller down the tray's corrugated ramp into the paint, then work it back and forth over the ramp to distribute the paint evenly. When the roller is fully loaded, you're ready to paint. Reload as soon as the roller becomes dry.

▼ To remove excess lint from a roller so you don't wind up with small hairs in the paint on your walls, roll the pile across a length of tape pulled taut before you begin.

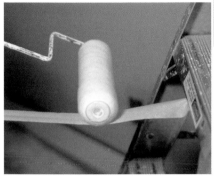

◄ Paint shouldn't be dripping off the roller, nor should there be dry spots.

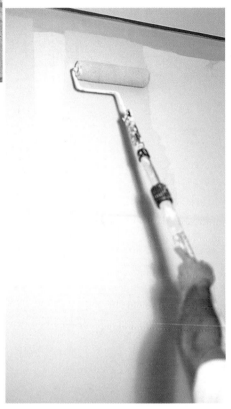

WORK IN SECTIONS Apply the paint in sections about 3 by 3 feet. Different painters describe their initial roll pattern as an N, W, or M—all ways of saying that you should create a zigzag of thick paint and then even out the finish by rolling up and down through the wet paint. Do a section at the top of the wall, then immediately move down and do the lower part. Run your roller down the wall. Once you've done that, leave the paint alone, even if you see bare areas. The second coat will cover those. If the day is unusually dry and your roller drags on the final step, work in narrow bands from the top of the wall to the bottom rather than in short sections 3 feet across.

▶ For the final pass, run the roller from the top to the bottom in a single pass to smooth out the transition between painted areas.

faux molding

WHEN YOU'RE USING A SOLID COLOR, you can get paint right up to the ceiling or baseboard by following the steps shown on this and previous pages. With decorative effects, however, it's not always easy to extend the finish evenly into a tight corner. Many of the projects in chapter 2 include specific tips that help. But you also have the option of a clever shortcut: After you complete the decorative finish, paint a solid band of color along the edges. Think of it as faux molding.

CLEANING UP
after a paint project

One advantage of careful preparation is that you have less mess to clean up afterward. Still, some cleanup is involved in all painting jobs, and it should begin as soon as possible after you finish each coat of paint.

Though it's considered acceptable to send rinse water from water-based paint down the drain, always remove as much excess as possible from your tools and containers before you use water. You might even treat roller covers and brushes as one-project tools so that you don't generate a lot of dirty water.

■ Between coats, cover tools and containers tightly with plastic so there's no need to rinse.

■ At the end of the job, scrape containers with a plastic spatula like one you'd use in a kitchen. If you will be reusing rollers, scrape them with the curved section of a painter's 5-in-1 tool. For paint pads, use the front edge of the 5-in-1.

■ Remove excess paint from brushes by working the bristles back and forth on old newspaper. Use the same trick to remove residue left after you have scraped rollers and paint pads.

■ Wash out the remaining paint with warm water and a little laundry detergent. If bits of paint remain in a brush, comb the bristles with a wire comb made for this purpose or

with a wire brush. Comb from the ferrule toward the tips.

■ Shake out excess water and allow tools to dry thoroughly before you store them. Line up bristles in their original direction while they are still damp. Protect them during storage by putting brushes back into their original cardboard holders.

After the first coat of paint, leave masking tape or paper over doorways and in other places where the paint edge won't be visible. But remove masking between coats where the paint edge shows, such

as along baseboards and the vertical trim at doorways and windows. Because the tape or paper is likely to have wet paint smeared on it, dump it directly into a garbage container, not onto your drop cloth.

LEFTOVER PAINT OR GLAZE You'll probably want to store leftover paint for touch-ups later. Put a dot of paint on the lid or label depending on how you will view the can while it is on a storage shelf. Then write down the room where you used the paint. Clean the rim of the can and

▲ Immediately after you remove masking materials, inspect the underlying areas for spots where paint seeped in. Clean off the drips with a barely damp cloth wrapped over a painter's 5-in-1 tool, not a bulky rag, so that you don't risk marring the painted wall. Though water-based paint dries to the touch in as little as an hour, it remains fairly soft for a long time afterward.

lid so that you can get a good seal when you tap down the lid. Store water-based products where they won't freeze, as repeated freezing and thawing can ruin the formula.

To dispose of water-based paint, including what you scraped off your tools, stir clay-based kitty litter into the paint until it is no longer fluid. After that, you can dispose of the container with your household trash.

If you end up with large quantities of paint you don't want, call your local solid-waste agency or garbage-collection service to inquire about nonprofit agencies or other groups that might be able to use it. Some communities mix unwanted paint and use it to cover graffiti. In others, artists recycle leftovers for neighborhood projects.

▼ To dispose of leftover water-based finishes with your household garbage, first stir in enough kitty litter so the waste is no longer liquid.

safety

WATER-BASED PAINTS don't pose the fire hazard that some oil-based products do, and they release far less fumes as they cure. However, most formulas still contain small amounts of solvents other than water, and some can trigger allergic reactions if you inhale them. The solvents can also dry out your skin if it is in contact with the paint for long periods. Open windows while you paint, or consider wearing a respirator designed to absorb fumes from water-based paint. When you tackle a decorative technique that requires your hands to be in contact with paint or glaze, wear disposable gloves.

For the least smelly, most environmentally benign paints, look for low-odor products that are also low in VOCs (volatile organic compounds), preferably with certification from an independent organization such as Green Seal. Avoid products with the words "warning" or "caution" on the label or with hazardous ingredients listed on the manufacturer's safety data sheet, which the store should be able to supply.

▲ Using water-based paints is particularly important in a child's room that must be occupied soon after it is painted.

CREATING
decorative effects

DECORATIVE EFFECTS BRING plain paint to life. Using the techniques shown in this chapter, you can create walls with subtle color variations that resemble parchment or suede, or give them the brassy look of bold diamonds or even gold leaf.

Feel free to mix and match the color schemes and materials shown for each faux and decorative effect. For example, you might follow the steps for creating stripes but add flourishes taken from another project, such as raised stenciling. Because many people find that color selection is the hardest part of painting, this chapter provides an array of inspirational color combinations for mottling, geometrics, dragging, and metallic effects.

You may want to start by exploring various ways to achieve a mottled look with glaze. This subtle blending of colors is a popular and easy decorative technique. You can use it by itself or combine it with more complex looks. Then test your skills with challenging projects such as venetian plaster, frottage, and marbling.

▶ Part of the fun of decorative painting is using familiar tools in unusual ways. Here, a standard feather duster is used to create a mottled look. See page 64 for the final result.

deciding on a project

With all the options for decorative painting, you may be stumped about which technique to try first. This chart shows a difficulty rating for each project in the book, key issues, and important considerations such as the initial wall texture needed. Some techniques can be done only on smooth surfaces, which means that if your walls have a texture, you'll need to skim-coat the surface first (see pages 178–179). Some projects will leave a texture, but to restore a smooth surface later on you can usually sand or skim-coat over it with dry-wall mud. All of the projects in this chapter assume that basic preparation has been done. This generally includes patching holes and applying the proper primer, steps that are detailed starting on page 174.

Category	Project	Difficulty*	Initial wall texture	Key issues
Mottled looks	Mottling with a rag, p. 58	2	Any	As with all mottling techniques, the main challenge is to maintain consistency across a wall. Step back occasionally to check your progress.
	Mottling with cheesecloth, p. 60	2	Any	Use high-quality cheesecloth and be sure to keep the material folded so edges aren't exposed; otherwise loose fibers may become caught in the glaze.
	Mottling with a brush, p. 62	2	Any	Allows you to complete the job with just one application tool.
	Mottling with a two-part roller, p. 63	1	Any	It's very quick, but because you use only paint it lacks the translucent quality of mottled effects created with glazes. The roller can't reach into tight corners.
	Mottling with a feather duster, p. 64	1	Any	Buy extra dusters so you can switch when one becomes too clogged with glaze.
	Mottling by rag rolling, p. 65	4	Smooth	Ensuring an even finish is difficult; your fingers tend to get in the way and cause the glaze to smudge.
	Rag rolling with a roller, p. 65	2	Smooth	It's very quick, but the roller can't reach into tight corners so you must either do those by hand or apply a band of solid paint there.
Geometric designs	Moiré stripes, p. 72	2–3	Smooth or light orange-peel texture	This project is easier if you stop at plain stripes. The full effect, with mottling and a moiré look, is more complicated.
	Limestone blocks, p. 75	3	Any	One set of blocks must be dry before you glaze adjoining ones. The technique looks great when applied to a textured surface, but the texture increases the chance that glaze will seep under the tape that separates the blocks, requiring you to touch up the lines with paint.
	Dry-brushed blocks, p. 78	4	Any	Allow plenty of time; initial blocks must dry before you paint adjoining areas.
	Diamonds, p. 80	4	Smooth or light orange-peel texture	Laying out the dividing lines and planning your painting sequence are more complicated than for blocks or stripes; it's easy to get mixed up.
Dragged effects	Strié, p. 88	2	Smooth or light orange-peel texture	Keeping lines straight takes a steady hand. The top and bottom edges are the most difficult; consider painting a solid line there. Leaves texture.
	Linen, p. 90	3	Smooth or light orange-peel texture	This has the same issues as with strié, but you must drag in two directions. Leaves texture.
	Small-scale combed designs, p. 92	1	Smooth	This is the easiest dragged effect because you comb only short distances in each swath. Leaves texture.
	Combed checks, p. 94	3	Smooth	You must drag in two directions, so expect some unevenness in the results. Leaves texture.
	Plaid, p. 97	3	Smooth	The design emerges when glaze is scraped off, so work in small sections; the surface can't get too dry to manipulate. May leave texture.
	Rolled squares, p. 98	3	Smooth or slight texture	Expect irregularities. Paint will inevitably migrate onto taped sections of the roller.

*1 = easiest, 4 = hardest

Category	Project	Difficulty*	Initial wall texture	Key issues
Stencils	Stenciled border, p. 106	1	Any	Apply over a smooth surface if you want crisp details on the stenciled design. On a textured surface, expect more irregularities.
	Raised stencil, p. 109	2	Any	Same issues as with border stencils. Painting the raised design is time-consuming. Leaves texture.
Plaster effects	Polished venetian plaster, p. 114	4	Smooth	Polishing changes the color as well as the sheen, so achieving a uniform surface is difficult. Expect variations. This can be painted over, but you'll loose the look of polished plaster.
	Multicolored venetian plaster, p. 116	1	Any	Step back occasionally to make sure you are applying a consistent mix of colors across the wall. Leaves texture.
	Stenciled venetian plaster, p. 118	2	Smooth	Allow enough drying time so you don't risk smudging a completed area when you go on to the next part of the pattern. Leaves texture.
	Embossed textures, p. 121	2	Any	Step back occasionally to make sure the effect is consistent across the wall. Leaves texture.
	Lace designs, p.123	1	Any	Step back occasionally to make sure you are applying the design consistently across the wall. Leaves texture.
	Plaster with mix-ins, p. 124	2	Any	Use a light touch when you glaze the surface so you don't dislodge the seeds. Leaves texture.
	Plaster with straw, p. 125	2	Any	The big challenge is to get the straw to adhere without covering it completely. Practice first. Step back occasionally to check for consistency. Leaves texture.
Special effects	Clouds, p. 128	1–3	Any	Generic clouds are easy to make. Creating a specific type is more difficult. Practice first.
	Wood graining, p. 130	3	Smooth	Practice until you can repeat the design fairly uniformly across a surface. This may require sanding to restore a smooth surface.
	Spattering, p. 132	1	Any	Big drips ruin the effect, so practice first to be sure the consistency of the paint and your spattering technique are well matched. This may require sanding to restore a smooth surface.
	Frottage, p. 134	3	Any	Avoid tackling too large an area at once, particularly in hot or dry weather, or the newsprint may stick to the wall. Leaves texture.
	Tissue paper texture, p. 136	2	Smooth or light orange-peel texture	Don't expect this texture to mask underlying problems in the wall, such as patches that have a different texture than the surrounding surface. The tissue is thin, so irregularities will still show. Leaves texture. To restore a smooth surface, dampen a small area and test whether the wallpaper adhesive softens enough so you can scrape off the texture. If that doesn't work, sand or skim-coat with drywall mud.
	Marbling, p. 139	4	Smooth	It takes practice to apply the different colors in a way that will create a realistic look.
Metallic effects	Brushed metal, p. 146	1	Smooth	Step back occasionally to make sure your technique stays consistent across the wall. Leaves texture.
	Hammered metal, p. 148	2	Smooth	Allow plenty of time, because you can't paint adjoining sections until initial areas dry.
	Metallic pot, p. 150	3	Any	Apply the patina chemicals sparingly until you see how much color change occurs. You can always add more, but you can't undo tarnish once it occurs. Use an acrylic primer/sealer before you repaint.
	Gold leaf, p. 154	4	Smooth	Sheets are thin and tear easily, so work carefully and brush lightly as you press pieces into the adhesive.
Antique effects	China crackle, p. 162	2	Not for walls	This type of crackle material creates a lightly textured pattern. Use on furniture, woodwork, etc. Leaves slight texture. Sand to restore a smooth surface.
	Aged crackle, p. 164	3	Not for walls	Best on horizontal surfaces because it tends to slip on vertical areas. Adds more texture than china crackle. Sand or plug indentations with wood filler to restore a smooth surface.
Lime paint and wash	Lime paint, p. 168	1	Any	This works best over a thin layer of drywall mud. If the wall is already painted, you will probably need to prime it first. Check the label.
	Lime wash, p. 171	1	Any	Can be used alone to produce texture that's hazy white. If you want color, coat the dried texture material with tinted glaze. Wall irregularities, such as patches that have a different texture than the surrounding wall, will show. For best results, apply over a smooth or uniformly textured surface. Leaves texture.

*1 = easiest, 4 = hardest

MOTTLED
looks

Mottled looks go by different names, including color wash, antique glaze, parchment, and leather. But they're all variations of the same effect: translucent color or colors swirling over a base color, resulting in a mixture that varies in intensity from one spot to another.

▲ To produce a mottled look with crisp, random lines, apply glaze with a twisted rag using a technique known as rag rolling. Although you can select paint and glaze colors just a few shades apart, this room gets its charm from the sharper contrast of blue glaze over off-white paint.

There are many ways to achieve this look, as you will see in the projects that follow. If you choose base paint and glaze that are close in color, the effect will be subtle. A dark glaze over a light-colored base, or vice versa, makes a bolder statement, especially if the hues are different. Whatever the colors, you can tone down the effect by blending the edges of the glaze well. If you want a livelier look, go easy on the blending. You can brush on the glaze, or dab it on with a variety of tools, including sea wool sponges and feather dusters.

◄ An urn filled with pumpkins gains much of its beauty from the differing colors of the pumpkin rinds. The mottled paint on the wall works for the same reason: It blends gold tones in a way that seems natural and alive.

▶ Mottling with two colors of a relatively opaque glaze produced this effect. For the decorative bands near the ceiling, the painter used each color separately.

◄ Because mottling combines different colors, you can use it to tie a room's shades together. Here, the pink in the floor tiles reappears in the glaze on the walls.

ensuring an even finish

WHATEVER THE TOOL, the hardest part of creating a mottled effect is getting it to look even throughout the room. These strategies help:

■ If you are working with a partner, have one person apply the glaze and the other person blend it throughout the room.

■ Step back occasionally and look at the overall effect. Glaze remains soft for an extended period, so you can wipe it off and start over if you really dislike what you see.

■ Avoid overlapping glaze onto areas you have just completed, as doing so will leave some areas with twice as much glaze as others.

■ Work in sections with irregular shapes. If you work in square or rectangular areas that line up, any overlaps will be much more visible.

mottling with a rag

There are several methods for producing a mottled look, and each results in a slightly different effect. For this project, cotton rags cut from old T-shirts were used to blend the glaze. Using a rag gives you the option of imprinting a network of small, random lines on the wall or creating a softer look without lines. It all depends on how you fold the cloth and whether you mostly rub or pounce with it.

This project uses a deep-tinted glaze over a much lighter base coat. To create even deeper color, start with a darker base, or coat a larger percentage of the wall with glaze.

The glaze must be fairly translucent if you want hints of the background color to show even in areas where the glaze is most prominent. For glaze tinted with paint, that means adding no more than 1 part paint to 4 parts glaze. Add more glaze if you want a more translucent finish, but don't boost the concentration of paint or the mixture will be too opaque and too likely to dry before you have had time to create the mottled look.

materials and tools

- Base paint (eggshell sheen)
- Glaze
- Paint or universal colorants to tint glaze
- Roller with cover
- 3-inch chip brush
- Cotton T-shirt rags
- Painter's 5-in-1 tool

1. Apply two coats of the base color in an eggshell sheen.

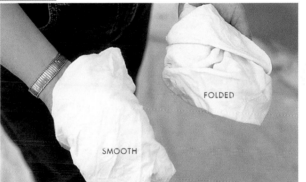

▲ **2.** When the base coat is dry, prepare a medium glaze (see page 29). Start in a corner and work in areas about 2 by 2 feet. Roll on the glaze in random patches so that you skip some areas. Keep the roller an inch or two from the corner.

▲ **3.** Work quickly so that the glaze doesn't dry before you complete adjoining areas. With a chip brush, dab some of the rolled-on glaze into the corner of the wall where you are working. You could mask the adjoining wall with painter's tape to keep it clean. But if you do this while mottling, you may wind up with a line where glaze pooled against the tape.

▲ **4.** Wad a piece of an old T-shirt into a pad. If you want faint lines on your finished wall, arrange the rag so that folds show on the working surface. If you want the colors to blend seamlessly, as in this project, smooth the cloth so the pad has no ridges.

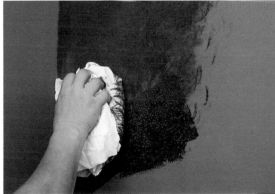

▲ **5.** With the cloth, dab and rub the glaze until it coats the surface in a way you like. If you're in doubt, remove more glaze than you think you want. Once the glaze is dry, you can always add a second coat. As your rag becomes saturated, refold it to expose a fresh surface. Wipe off any smears on the adjoining wall with a damp cloth wrapped around a drywall knife or a painter's 5-in-1 tool (see page 50). This allows you to reach just to the corner.

▲ **6.** Repeat this process for adjoining areas. The finished effect will show swirls of color that blend into one another.

mottling with cheesecloth

This and other mottling techniques shown on the following pages are similar to mottling with a rag, so first read the instructions on pages 58–59 for tips about general issues, such as how big an area to tackle, how to spread the glaze into corners, and how to clean smudges off adjoining walls.

Each method of mottling does have its unique issues, however. With cheesecloth, the light-as-air weave allows you to create very subtle effects. But the loose weave increases the risk that stray bits of thread will wind up in the glaze. To avoid that, form the cloth into a pouf, as shown on the next page.

materials and tools

- Base paint (eggshell sheen)
- Glaze
- Paint or universal colorants to tint glaze
- Roller with cover
- 3-inch chip brush
- Cheesecloth
- Cotton T-shirt rags
- Painter's 5-in-1 tool

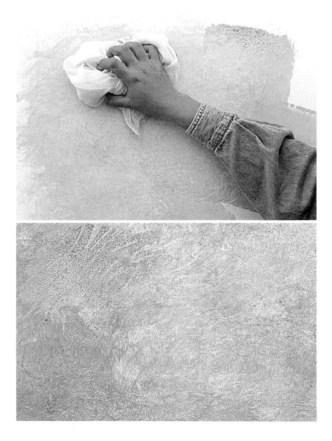

▲ **1.** Apply two coats of base paint. When the final coat is dry, brush or roll on glaze in random patches.

▶ **2.** Form cheesecloth into a pouf so no loose threads are exposed.
a) Cut a piece several feet long and drape it in a single layer over one hand.
b) Gather the loose ends and fold the cloth upward in accordion pleats.
c) Tuck the gathered section under the cloth that's covering your hand, forming a thick pad. Smooth the surface if you want the glaze to look uniform. Make small folds if you want the glaze to look textured.

▶ **3.** If you want the glaze and base colors to blend seamlessly, rub the surface with a smooth pouf to distribute the glaze. If you want a textured surface, repeatedly press down and lift up with a wrinkled pouf so that the folds in the cheesecloth leave small lines in the glaze.

4. Refold the cheesecloth as the fibers become saturated with glaze. When there are no fresh sections of cloth, switch to another piece.

▶ **5.** The final effect using a wrinkled pouf and a rubbing motion.

mottling with a brush

When you use a brush to apply glaze, you can leave obvious bristle marks if you wish. Or you can work the glaze until individual strokes disappear and the glaze becomes more like a colored cloud, with areas of more intense color blending seamlessly into areas where the glaze is lighter.

materials and tools

- Base paint (eggshell sheen)
- Glaze
- Paint or universal colorants to tint glaze
- Wide, thick brush
- 3-inch chip brush
- Cotton T-shirt rags
- Painter's 5-in-1 tool

▲ **1.** Apply two coats of base paint. When the final coat is dry, prepare a medium glaze (see page 29). With a wide, thick brush, apply patches of glaze to the base coat. Immediately brush out the glaze to distribute it over the bare areas.

2. Use a chip brush to move some of the glaze into the corner, as shown in step 3 on page 59. Wipe smears off the adjoining wall with a damp rag wrapped around a painter's 5-in-1 tool (see page 50).

▶ **3.** The final result shows subtle brush marks or not, depending on how much you brush the glaze.

mottling with a two-part roller

With a special roller and paint tray, you can apply two colors of paint at the same time. The effect is jarring at first, but if you roll back and forth in random directions, the colors blend and create a mottled look. Because you use only paint, the finish lacks the translucent quality that glaze offers. The trade-off, though, is speed, as you don't need separate base and glaze coats.

materials and tools

- Two-part roller with tray
- Wall paint in two colors (any sheen)
- Painter's tape
- Newspaper
- Chip brush
- Cotton T-shirt rags

1. Apply painter's tape along the top, bottom, and side edges of the first wall you will paint.

▲ **2.** Pour the two colors of paint into separate sections of the tray. Load the roller by moving it back and forth into the paint and across the raised section of the tray.

▶ **3.** Roll back and forth in different directions on several sheets of newspaper until the paint colors blend on the roller. Duplicating what would happen over time, this break-in helps ensure that the first wall section you paint will look similar to sections painted later. (You need to roll onto newsprint only at the beginning of the job.)

▶ **4.** Reload the roller and begin painting the wall. Roll back and forth in random directions.

5. Use the chip brush to move some of the paint into corners where the roller doesn't reach. Dab to blend colors so the look resembles the rest of the wall. Remove the painter's tape when you finish the wall. With a damp rag, clean off any smears on the ceiling or baseboard. You don't have to worry about smears on adjoining walls if you will paint over them.

▶ **6.** The final effect shows how the colors blend. Wait for one wall to dry before you paint the next. Tightly cover the roller and tray with plastic while you wait.

mottling with a feather duster

This technique produces a mottled look marked with distinct lines and highlights. You can use a relatively opaque glaze. The high proportion of paint to glaze will cause the finish to dry quickly, but that's fine because you don't need to work the glaze as much as you do with some other mottling techniques. Choose paint and glaze in similar tones if you want a subdued look.

You will probably need more than one feather duster, because the feathers become clogged as glaze dries on them. In a typical room, 10 by 10 feet, you might need five. Feather dusters sold at paint stores should be colorfast, but always test them to make sure dye on the feathers doesn't transfer into the glaze.

materials and tools

- Base paint (eggshell sheen)
- Glaze
- Paint or universal colorant to tint glaze
- Plastic bowl or other wide container
- Several feather dusters
- Newspaper
- Painter's tape
- Cotton T-shirt rags
- Painter's 5-in-1 tool

1. Apply two coats of base paint. When the final coat is dry, use painter's tape to mask the edges of the first wall you will embellish.

▼ **2.** Prepare an opaque or medium glaze (see page 29). Pour some of the mixture into the wide container. Dip the tips of the feather duster into the glaze, then dab the glaze onto scrap newspaper a few times before you begin to apply the glaze to the wall. This helps ensure an even look. Start in one corner and work on a section about 2 by 3 feet. Pounce in and out rather than rub. Each time you reload the duster, pounce in a few areas several inches apart. Then fill in between them with glaze left on the duster.

▼ **3.** Go over the area a second time to make the effect more uniform.

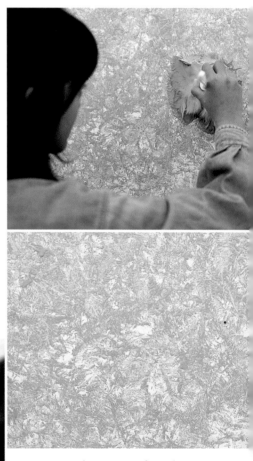

▲ **4.** Repeat this process for adjoining areas along the corner. Then remove the painter's tape there. With a damp rag, clean up any smears. Proceed to glaze adjoining sections until you complete the wall. The final effect shows a random pattern.

mottling by rag rolling

Rag rolling produces a mottled look with distinct lines. There are two ways to do it—with gloved hands and a twisted rag, or with a specialized roller. Rollers don't reach into corners or narrow sections near doorways or windows, so you will probably need to do parts by hand even if you opt for a roller for the big expanse of a wall.

materials and tools

- Base paint (eggshell sheen)
- Glaze
- Paint or universal colorant to tint glaze
- Painter's tape
- Cotton T-shirt rags
- Disposable gloves

1. Apply two coats of base paint. When the final coat is dry, tape off all areas you do not want to paint. Also tape along adjoining walls because rag-rolling deposits far more glaze into corners than other mottling methods do.

▲ **2.** Prepare an opaque or medium glaze (see page 29). Put on gloves. Dunk a dry rag into the glaze and twist the cloth so that it resembles a thick, short rope.

▼ **3.** Roll the rag across the wall in random directions. When the marks become faint, reload the cloth with more glaze and continue rolling; but if your rag becomes too saturated, it will slip on the surface and smear the glaze. Also, along a corner, avoid using a freshly loaded rag because excess glaze may drip. Instead, push a fairly dry cloth gently into the corner.

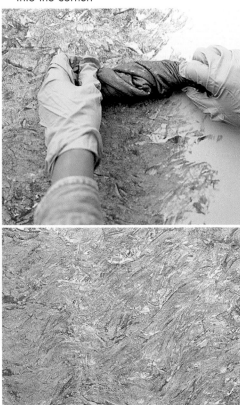

▲ **4.** The final result shows a random pattern in the glaze.

rag rolling with a roller

TO CREATE THIS LOOK with a roller, use a specialized tool that consists of a cylinder with a cloth cover and end caps. The cloth cover is twisted to create a series of folds that leave their imprint in the glaze. With the roller, you can produce a network of diagonal lines. But if you're working in small areas where the roller won't fit, you'll need to glaze some sections by hand. In this case, roll in random directions so the two areas blend.

CHOOSING COLORS
for mottled looks

Mottled looks run the gamut from subtle to vivid. Many people want a "Tuscan look," a "parchment look," or "something that resembles leather." All of these can be accomplished with the right combination of base paint and glaze colors.

BASE PAINT　　GLAZE

BASE PAINT　　GLAZE

BASE PAINT

GLAZE

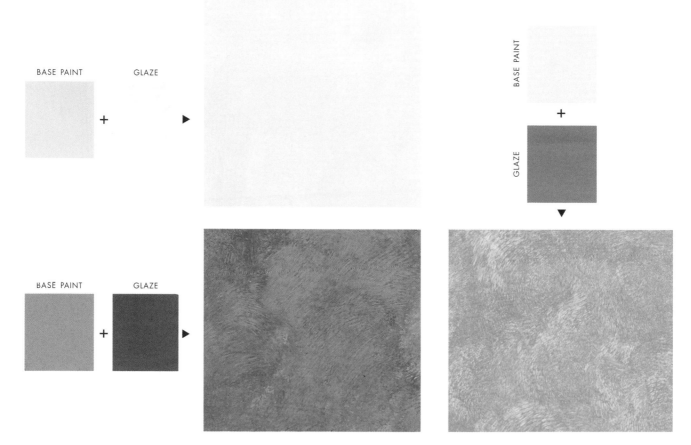

BASE PAINT　　GLAZE

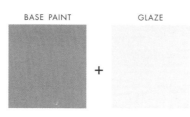

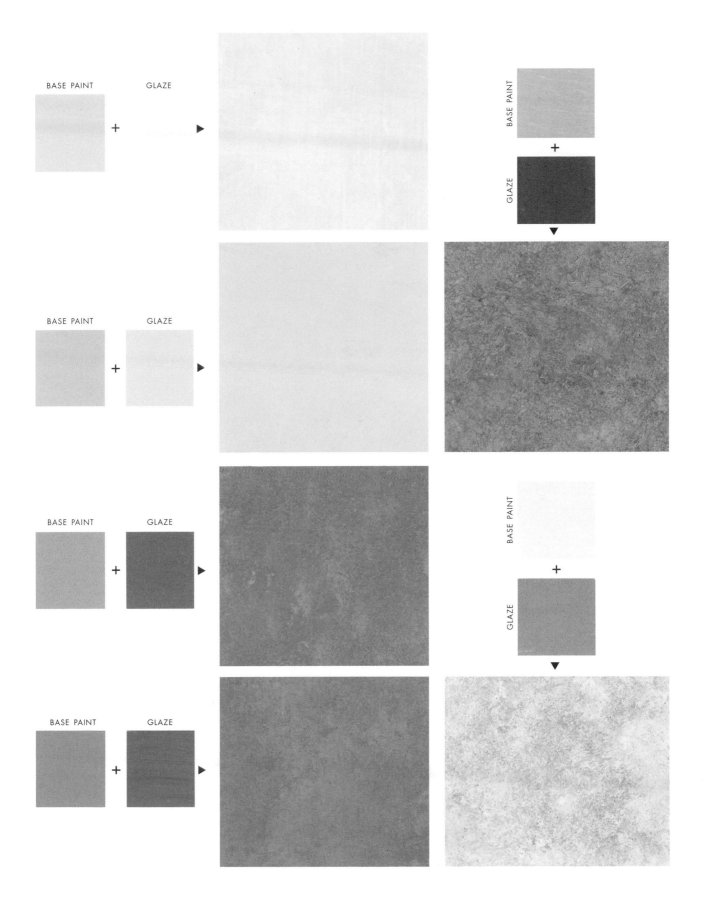

BASE PAINT   GLAZE

BASE PAINT   GLAZE

BASE PAINT

+

GLAZE

BASE PAINT   GLAZE

BASE PAINT

+

GLAZE

BASE PAINT   GLAZE

GEOMETRIC DESIGNS:
blocks, stripes, and diamonds

Geometric designs can be bold and playful, or demure and conservative, depending on how much their colors contrast. To create a whispered effect, paint the designs in a single color but use different sheens, such as flat and semigloss, or vary the glaze colors only slightly from one section to another. For more drama, opt for colors that contrast vividly.

◄ To simulate the look of limestone blocks, these walls were first painted light yellow. The block design was laid out and marked off with tape, and a darker yellow glaze was applied to alternate rows. The grout lines were painted in freehand at the end. To top off the wall, the painter also stenciled in crown molding.

If you're creating blocks or diamonds, your decision about whether to have sections touch one another or remain separated greatly affects how much time you will need to complete the job. If they touch, you can glaze or paint only every other section at one time. You must remove the painter's tape along edges, wait for the finish to dry, and reposition the tape before you can coat remaining sections. However, if you let the base paint show between sections or if you add dividing lines later, perhaps as faux grout, you need to apply tape only once and you can paint or glaze without interruption.

◄ Creative use of geometrics turns a sunroom floor into a multipurpose play space. To lay out and paint designs like this, you can adapt the stripe and block projects shown in this chapter for the main elements and paint the remaining details freehand.

▲ If you want to duplicate a woven plaid with paint, as the designs on the walls and dresser of this bedroom do, combine the steps used to lay out blocks (pages 75–79) with the technique for creating a linen look (pages 90–101).

▲ Narrow stripes emphasize a recurring stylistic feature of this room: its arches.

▶ The direction of stripes makes a big difference in their effect. Wide, horizontal lines set a Bauhaus theme for this room and make it seem wider than it is.

laying out a geometric design

With any geometric design, the challenge is not so much in the actual painting as in the measuring, marking, and keeping track of the right painting sequence.

If you are painting a single wall, you will probably want the design to fit evenly within the space. To calculate the width of stripes or the height and width of blocks and diamonds, divide the wall's width or height by the number of designs you want there. Or use the math-light method described at right. When you've settled on dimensions that seem to work, test the result by cutting the shape from newsprint or brown paper. Tape this pattern on the wall. Stand back and make sure you like the proportions. Then proceed to mark the walls.

If you want a design to wrap around all the walls in a room, you're unlikely to find a size that divides evenly into the width of all the walls. You have two choices: adjust the sizes slightly so the shapes fit evenly in each space, or extend the design around corners. If you take the latter approach, begin measuring and marking in an inconspicuous place, such as on the wall where you enter, so that any irregularity in the final pieces won't be as noticeable.

MATH-LIGHT DIVISION To determine what width fits in even multiples across a wall, you can measure the wall and divide by the number of spaces you want to create. But this usually leaves a fraction that's hard to deal with. Try the method shown here.

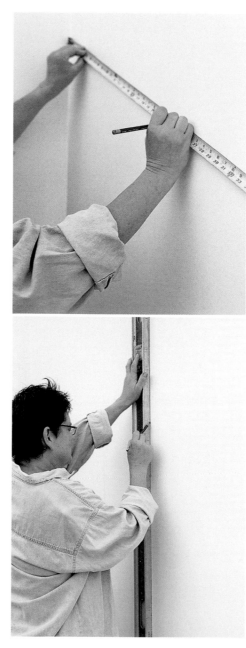

◀ **1.** Extend your tape measure across the space at an angle, rather than horizontally, so that the end point shows a number that can be divided evenly by the number of sections you want. For example, if a wall is 89 inches wide and you want stripes that are 9 inches wide, tip the tape measure so the end point is at 90 inches. With a pencil, make a light vertical mark at each division. In this example, that would be every 10 inches.

◀ **2.** With a level, extend those marks for the height of the wall.

tip TO MEASURE into a tight corner with a tape measure, add the length of the tape's housing, often 3 inches, to the number that shows on the tape. Bending the tape into a corner isn't as accurate.

USING PAINTER'S TAPE Painter's tape helps ensure crisp, straight edges in geometric designs, but it isn't foolproof. Sometimes when you pull the tape off, you discover that some of the finish seeped underneath, leaving a ragged line. To avoid this problem, follow the sequence below. It's shown with stripes but works with blocks and diamonds as well.

1. Paint the wall with two coats of the lighter color (yellow in this example). Let each coat dry as the label recommends.

2. Measure and mark the walls, then align painter's tape along areas you want to darken. Keep the tape on the light-colored side of the line, where you don't want to add paint. Press the tape down tightly.

▼ **3.** To ensure a crisp line, especially on textured surfaces, paint edges of the tape with the light-colored paint. This way, if paint seeps under the tape, it will be the same color as the paint you are trying to protect.

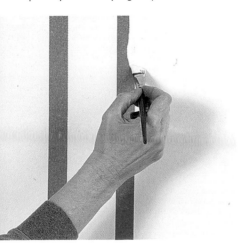

▲ **4.** Once that paint is dry, roll on the darker color.

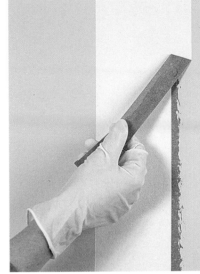

▲ **5.** Pull off the tape at a 45-degree angle to the wall.

marking tools

YOU HAVE A CHOICE of marking tools when you lay out geometric designs. An important factor is whether you will be able to cover or erase the marks you make, or whether they will show in the final finish.

■ If you will cover the marks with paint, you can use a standard No. 2 pencil. Trace against a straightedge, such as a level.

■ If you will cover the marks with painter's tape, carpenter's chalk usually works best, especially over long distances. Stretching the string taut and snapping the chalky coating onto the wall is easier if a partner holds one end, but you can also hook the line over a small nail that's partially set. After you apply painter's tape along the line, brush off any exposed chalk. Then, after the wall is painted, clean off the remaining chalk. You can also use a No. 2 pencil, but make light marks and erase them later.

■ If you will cover the marks with glaze, use a colored pencil in a shade that won't be noticeable. You can't erase pencil marks or brush off chalk lines once they are covered with glaze.

moiré stripes

Moiré originally referred to the irregular, wavy texture seen on silk fabric after it passed through hot, ribbed rollers. The texture made the cloth shimmer even more than usual. The same technique eventually became popular for other fabrics and materials, including wallpaper, during the Victorian era. This project uses a graining tool called a rocker to create a similar effect on alternating stripes.

The design is perfect for a Victorian setting, of course, but in pale colors it would also suit a dining room or a fairly formal living room in any style of home. In a bright color such as hot pink, it would liven up a child's bedroom.

materials and tools

- Base paint (eggshell sheen)
- Glaze
- Paint or universal colorant to tint glaze
- Painter's tape
- Level
- Pencil or colored pencil
- Eraser
- Roller and cover (must fit within stripes) or a brush
- 3- or 4-inch chip brush
- Cheesecloth
- Rocker (graining tool)
- Cotton T-shirt rags

1. Apply two coats of the base color in an eggshell sheen, allowing each to dry as the label recommends.

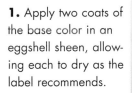

▲ **2.** Lay out the stripes (use the tips on pages 70–71) and apply tape along the lines in preparation for painting the darker color. To avoid confusion, place scraps of tape across sections that you want to skip.

▲ **3.** Paint the darker sections with a small roller or a brush. Remove the tape and let the paint dry.

▶ **4.** Erase any pencil marks that weren't painted over because they were hidden by tape.

◀ **5.** Apply new tape, this time covering the edges of the dark stripes. Working on one stripe at a time, brush a transparent glaze (see page 29) on the light stripes.

▶ **6.** With a length of cheesecloth gathered into a pouf, rub the glaze to create a mottled effect. If glaze gets on the darker stripes, wipe it off gently with a barely damp cloth. Remove the tape and allow the glaze to dry. This should take just a short time.

◀ **7.** Reapply the tape where it was in step 2. Prepare a medium glaze (see page 29). Working on one stripe at a time, brush the tinted glaze over the dark paint.

▶ **8.** Immediately go over the stripe with the rocker, working from the top down. As its name implies, rock it up and down as you pull it along. If stripes are wider than the rocker, go over each area with multiple passes, but vary how much you move forward at each rocking motion so that identical lines don't appear next to each other.

◀ **9.** Clean the rocker after each pass by wiping it on a barely damp cloth.

▼ **10.** When the glaze is dry, remove the tape and enjoy the final result.

customizing this project

YOU CAN ADAPT this project, like many in this book, to suit your preferences. If you want unadorned stripes, for example, stop at step 4. For solid stripes interspersed with mottled stripes, stop at step 7. Or if you want to speed the work by applying the tape just once, paint the dark stripes, remove the tape, and then create a mottled effect over the entire wall.

limestone blocks

This project shows an efficient way to create the look of limestone blocks separated by thin mortar joints. As a faux project, it's one of the easiest stone looks to create. Unlike others involving geometric patterns, this requires tape to be applied just once. You can add glaze layers and colors as many times as you wish if your initial efforts seem too light or unrealistic.

Masking tape just ¼ inch wide is worth tracking down for this project because it's what determines the width of the mortar joints. Tape sold at paint stores typically is at least ½ inch wide. While it will work, the painted joints are likely to look a bit clunky. Look for the skinny type at automobile parts stores, which sell it for masking cars when they are being pinstriped.

materials and tools

- Base paint (eggshell sheen)
- Glaze
- Several colors of paint or universal colorant to tint glaze
- ¼-inch-wide masking tape
- Level
- Pencil or colored pencil
- Eraser
- Sea-wool sponge
- Cheesecloth and/or cotton rags

1. Apply two coats of base paint and allow each coat to dry as the label recommends.

▶ **2.** Lay out the design using a level and a pencil. Consider blocks sketched in two sizes, some twice as long as others. Draw faint lines.

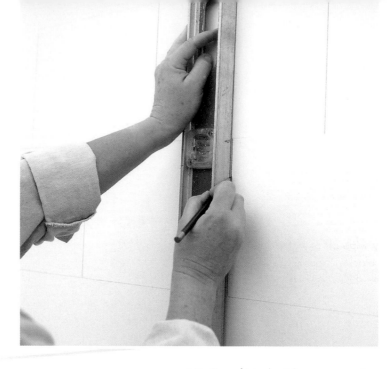

◀ **3.** Press ¼-inch-wide tape over the lines. Aim to have the line centered under the tape, but don't worry if the tape strays a bit. Masonry isn't perfect either.

▶ **4.** Prepare a medium glaze (see page 29). Dip a sea-wool sponge into a little of the glaze. You should pick up just enough to color the outermost part of the sponge, not soak it.

◀ **5.** Working on one block at a time, pat the sponge on the wall to transfer some of the glaze. Repeat with different colors of glaze, but wipe the sponge off whenever you switch so that you don't muddy the colors.

▲ **6.** Quickly wipe off any glaze that gets into adjoining blocks. Though you will eventually apply glaze there, if smudges around the edges dry now, they will look like smudges when you're done.

▲ **7.** Go over the glaze with a cheesecloth pouf to blend the colors slightly. Don't overwork the glaze, however, or you will ruin its textured look.

8. Repeat steps 5, 6, and 7 on every other block. Skip blocks so that you are working next to dry sections where you can wipe off smudges.

▲ **9.** When the glazed blocks are dry, go back to the blocks you skipped. As you work, wipe off any fresh glaze that smears over onto the completed blocks.

10. Step back and inspect your work. If the blocks seem too uniform or if the overall effect is too light, add glaze wherever you wish. Continue working next to blocks that are dry.

▲ **11.** When you're satisfied with the color, gently pull off the tape at a 45-degree angle to the wall. Follow up by erasing any pencil marks that were covered by the tape.

◀ **12.** The final result.

dry-brushed blocks

The richly textured blocks on this wall result from feathery strokes with a brush that's barely damp with metallic paint. The technique, known as dry brushing, works fine with standard paint and glazes, but it's especially well suited to mica-rich metallic paints, which are virtually impossible to apply in a uniform coat except with a sprayer. With a dry-brushed finish, you're supposed to see the brushstrokes, so uniformity is not an issue.

The initial steps are the same as those for any project that involves geometric designs. You need to measure and mark, then apply painter's tape to ensure crisp lines along each section. This project differs from the others in this section, however, in that it uses a random arrangement of blocks, some of which overlap others. You don't have to figure out a precise width or height that will fit evenly in your space. But you still need to ensure that all the lines are level or plumb and that the various block sizes relate well to one another and to the scale of your room.

materials and tools

- Base paint (eggshell sheen)
- Metallic or other paint in several colors
- Glaze (optional)
- Disposable plastic bowls or other containers to hold glaze

- Painter's tape
- Painter's 5-in-1 tool or drywall knife
- Level
- Pencil
- 3- or 4-inch chip brush
- Cotton T-shirt rags

1. If you're using metallic paint, make sure the surface is smooth so it reflects light well. For instructions on how to smooth out a textured wall, see pages 178–179. If you patch or skim-coat it, apply primer to the entire wall and allow the paint to dry.

2. Apply two coats of base paint in an eggshell sheen. Allow each coat to dry for the time specified on the label.

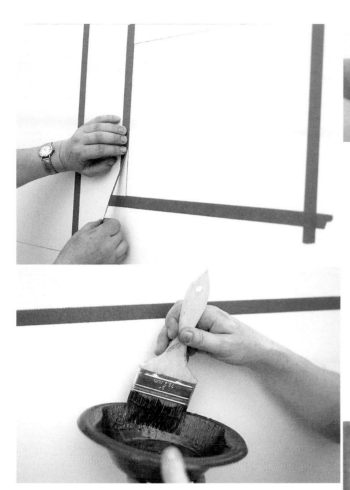

▲ **3.** Using a pencil and a level, lightly draw the design on the wall. You might want to work out a plan beforehand on graph paper. Put felt pads on the back of your level so you don't scratch the wall.

◄ **4.** Apply tape around the perimeter of isolated squares. Tape goes on the outside of the line.

◄ **5.** Mix paint and glaze in equal proportions, as shown here, or use undiluted paint if you want it opaque. Pour some of it into a container that's wider than your brush. An inexpensive chip brush 3 or 4 inches wide works well for this project. Dip the bristles only slightly into the paint or glaze.

▶ **6.** With light strokes, brush the paint or glaze onto a block. It will look splotchy, but don't worry. You can add more until you're satisfied, but leave some of the base showing so that you can see the brush marks. In a similar manner, paint the other blocks you have taped off, but use a variety of colors. Wipe the brush on clean rags if it becomes saturated with paint or glaze. Use a clean, dry brush when you change colors.

◄ **7.** When the first set of blocks is dry, remove the tape and put up fresh tape so you can paint the remaining areas. This tape goes on top of the sections you just painted. If you need to paint around a square that's already painted, ensure a crisp corner by tearing the overlapping tape at a 45-degree angle, as if it were a mitered picture frame.

8. If you are using metallic paint, brush on a clear, glossy finish such as shellac or acrylic to enhance the sheen.

diamonds

A diamond design is a bit more complicated to lay out than other geometric patterns because the edges run at an angle. However, the process gets easier once you realize that the tips of the diamonds sit on a grid of verticals and horizontals. The trick is to locate the positions of the tips, then draw the lines. Once you've done that, diamonds are as easy to paint as blocks.

Just as with blocks, plan on painting the diamonds over several work sessions. You can paint only every other block in one session. Then those must dry before you paint the sections in between.

This project features a dot of paint to embellish spots where the diamonds meet. Besides adding interest to the design, this helps mask any spots where the tips don't precisely meet. Instead of painted dots, you might also consider using upholstery tacks or small stenciled designs.

materials and tools

- Base paint (eggshell sheen)
- Glaze
- Paint or universal colorants to tint glaze
- Painter's tape
- Level
- Carpenter's chalk line
- Pencil or colored pencil
- Sheets of construction paper
- Cheesecloth and/or cotton rags

1. Paint the wall with two coats of the base color in an eggshell sheen. Allow each coat to dry as the label recommends.

▶ **2.** Use the math-light division method described on page 70 to determine the height of diamonds that will fit evenly between the top of the base-board and the ceiling (or the bottom of the crown molding). Using a level and a pencil, transfer the division marks to the sides of the walls. Repeat this process horizontally, transferring marks to the top and bottom of the wall.

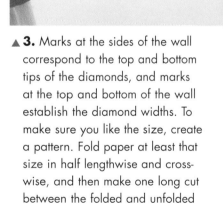

▲ **3.** Marks at the sides of the wall correspond to the top and bottom tips of the diamonds, and marks at the top and bottom of the wall establish the diamond widths. To make sure you like the size, create a pattern. Fold paper at least that size in half lengthwise and cross-wise, and then make one long cut between the folded and unfolded edges to create a diamond shape.

▲ **4.** Hold the diamond to the wall or tape it in place so you can step back and check the effect.

tip DIAMONDS USUALLY LOOK BEST when they are 1½ to 2 times as tall as they are wide.

◄5. Assuming you like the size, create the angled lines that mark the edges of the diamonds. Starting in one corner, use a chalk line to connect the lowest mark on that sidewall with the first mark against the baseboard. Continue connecting the marks in that way for the entire wall. If you get confused, just make sure the lines correspond to the shape of your paper pattern.

◄6. Apply tape around the perimeter of as many nonadjacent diamonds as possible. Because the tape rests partially on adjoining diamonds, you'll have to skip over many sections.

◄7. Prepare a medium glaze (see page 29). Brush or roll the glaze onto one diamond and immediately proceed to step 8.

tip EACH TIME you apply tape, brush off any exposed chalk. If you cover the chalk with glaze, you won't be able to remove it.

▲ **8.** With a cotton rag or a piece of cheesecloth gathered into a pouf, work the glaze until it has a pleasing mottled look. With a separate, barely damp rag, wipe off any glaze that gets on other diamonds. Repeat steps 7 and 8 on the other diamonds with tape around their edges.

▲ **9.** When the glaze is dry, remove the tape and put up fresh pieces so you can complete more of the diamonds. This tape runs over the first glaze in some spots. You may also want to mark diamonds that you will not glaze with short pieces of tape so you don't get confused.

10. Apply glaze to the rest of the diamonds that need it, then remove all the tape.

▶ **11.** Paint small circles of a contrasting color where the diamonds intersect. Use a circle template, or trace around a nickel or a quarter.

other diamond tricks

THERE ARE AT LEAST TWO other ways to paint diamonds.

■ Stencils for diamonds a few inches tall are readily available at craft stores and some paint stores.

■ Instead of taping individual diamonds, treat the diagonal lines created in step 5 as a layout for stripes. Roll tinted glaze over every other stripe that angles up from the bottom. When the glaze is dry, repeat the process with the stripes that angle down from the top. Glaze diamonds toward the end of the wall so they fit the pattern.

CHOOSING COLORS
for geometric designs

Geometric effects get their impact from contrasting colors or sheens. Rules that guide basic color theory help you achieve pleasing results (see page 20). For the liveliest look, select complementary colors. For a more toned-down look, use different tints of the same color.

BASE PAINT   GLAZE

BASE PAINT   GLAZE

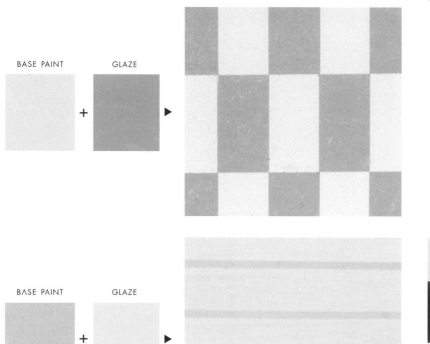

BASE PAINT

+

GLAZE

BASE PAINT   GLAZE

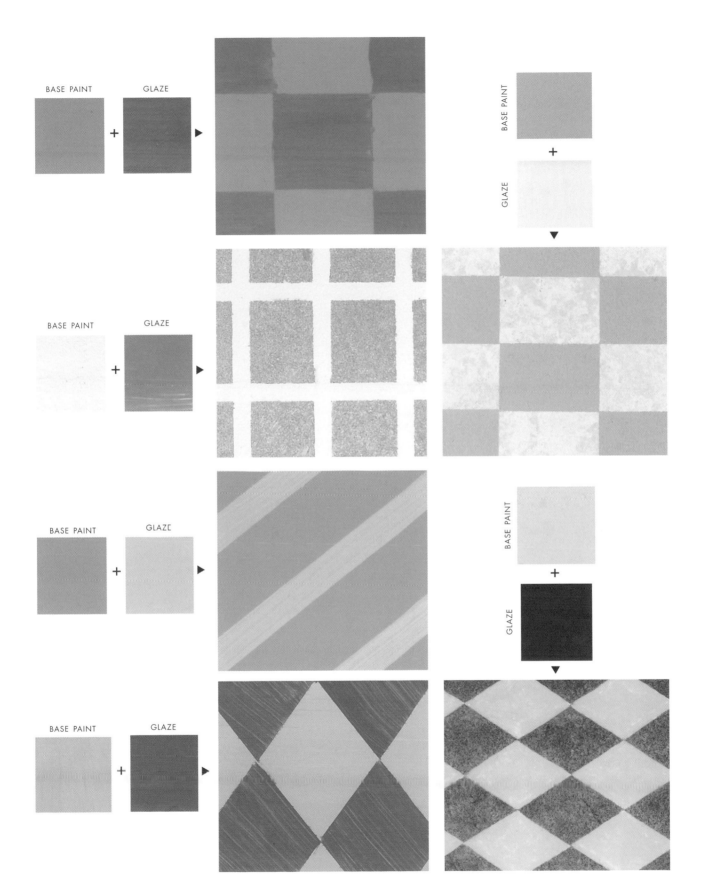

BASE PAINT   GLAZE   +

BASE PAINT   +   GLAZE

BASE PAINT   GLAZE   +

BASE PAINT   +   GLAZE

BASE PAINT   GLAZE   +

BASE PAINT   +   GLAZE

DRAGGED
effects

B y dragging a brush, comb, or other tool through freshly applied glaze, you can create a variety of textured finishes. Dragging a brush in one direction, usually vertically, produces an effect known as strié. It leaves the surface covered with fine striations, similar to what you'd expect in grass cloth. Dragging both vertically and horizontally creates the look of linen or denim. With the same techniques but different tools, you can produce bolder designs, including some that resemble handwoven gingham or handmade tiles, as you'll see in the following projects.

▲ The walls of this girl's bedroom were glazed to create a subtle linen effect. This type of finish requires two applications of glaze. First roll on one coat, drag it vertically with a brush, and allow it to dry. Then apply the second coat and drag it horizontally.

▼ Dragging a comb with relatively large teeth through freshly applied glaze produces striking designs. To create waves like the ones in this ceiling, jiggle the tool while moving it through the glaze.

▲ Moving a fine-tooth comb or rocker through red glaze over an off-white background results in this interesting effect. A random pattern like this is simple to make, but it's worth practicing on a sample board first to help ensure a consistent look across the entire surface. Experiment while you are working on the practice board, not while you are glazing the wall.

▲ Combing vertically and horizontally produces a pattern that resembles handwoven cloth.

strié

Strié is the quintessential dragged finish, elegant and understated. Made with a dry brush run through glaze that's just been rolled onto a wall, this finish leaves the surface textured with fine parallel lines. Doing it well takes practice and a steady hand. A few wiggly lines are inevitable, and in fact there should be just enough variation to reveal that this is a handcrafted finish, not one made by a machine in a factory.

Because you have to step up and down to brush through the glaze, you might want to limit this finish to walls that are no more than 8 feet tall so that you can use a stepstool instead of a ladder. You can also use the technique to decorate cabinets and trim. When it's done on trim in appropriate colors, the finish even mimics vertical-grain fir, as shown on the door at right.

materials and tools

- Base paint (eggshell sheen)
- Glaze
- Paint or universal colorant to tint glaze
- Painter's tape
- Roller with cover
- Paint tray
- 3- and 4-inch chip brushes, or one chip brush and one strié brush
- Cotton T-shirt rags

tip IT'S DIFFICULT TO KEEP lines straight at the top and bottom of the wall. If these areas look messy despite your best efforts, cover them with a band of wooden molding or a stripe of paint (see page 49).

1. Apply two coats of the base color in an eggshell sheen. Allow each coat to dry as the label recommends.

2. Protect adjoining surfaces by applying painter's tape around the wall you will glaze first.

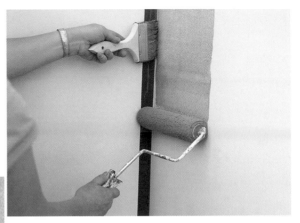

▲ **3.** Prepare an opaque or medium glaze (see page 29). Roll the glaze onto a section of the wall from top to bottom but no more than 2 feet wide. Stay back from the tape an inch or so. With a chip brush, work some of the glaze that's on the wall into the bare strip next to the tape. This keeps too much glaze from collecting there.

▲ **4.** Stand on a ladder or stepstool so you can reach the top of the wall. With a clean chip brush or a strié brush, rake downward through the glaze in a single long, steady motion. As you near the end of the area you can reach, lift the brush gradually so you don't leave an abrupt finish line.

▶ **5.** Get down from the ladder or stepstool. With a dry rag, wipe the brush free of glaze. Then position the bristles next to the baseboard and brush straight up. Extend this stroke into the area you brushed from the top. Again, lift the brush gradually to feather out the overlap.

6. Repeat steps 4 and 5 until you have brushed through the entire glazed area. Vary the height where you overlap strokes made from the top and the bottom so you don't see a line.

▶ **7.** Roll glaze onto an adjoining area, again about 2 feet wide. Slightly overlap the area you have already covered, but remove some of the excess by wiping through it quickly with the strié brush. Clean the bristles on a rag, then go over the area again to create the strié marks.

linen

A linen effect requires a process similar to strié, but you must apply two coats of glaze and brush them horizontally as well as vertically. Let the first coat dry before you apply the second so that you don't obliterate the first set of brushstrokes.

Be cautious about choosing this finish for unusually tall walls. The horizontal strokes are much easier if you don't have to climb down a ladder, move it, and climb back up every few feet. If your walls are taller than 8 feet—about the limit that you can reach from a stepstool—consider installing a band of horizontal trim to limit the area that you will decorate. A chair rail typically runs 3 or 4 feet off the floor, while a picture rail is usually even with the top of the trim above doors and windows. If you use either type of molding, you can create a linen look on just the lower section of the wall.

A specialty brush created the texture shown here. Other options are a 4-inch-wide chip brush and a wallpaper brush, which is typically about a foot wide.

materials and tools

- ◆ Base paint (eggshell sheen)
- ◆ Glaze
- ◆ Paint or universal colorant to tint glaze
- ◆ Painter's tape
- ◆ Roller with cover
- ◆ Paint tray
- ◆ Chip brush
- ◆ Linen weave brush or another dragging tool
- ◆ Cotton T-shirt rags

1. Apply two coats of the base color in an eggshell sheen, allowing each to dry.

2. Smooth painter's tape along all edges of the surface you will glaze first.

▶ **3.** Prepare a medium to opaque glaze (see page 29). Starting in a corner, roll it onto a vertical section about 2 feet wide. Keep the roller an inch or so from the corner and use a chip brush to smear some of the glaze across the gap.

▶ **4.** Immediately drag your brush through the glaze to create a pattern of parallel vertical lines. Feather out areas where you must overlap strokes that you make downward from a ladder or stepstool with those that you make upward from the floor. Wipe the brush often on a clean cloth.

5. Roll glaze onto the next section. Slightly overlap the area you just brushed. Immediately rake through the new glaze with the brush. Stop often to clean the bristles. When you have glazed the entire surface, allow the finish to dry at least overnight.

◀ **6.** Roll on the second layer of glaze in horizontal bands about 2 feet high. Immediately go over each area with a brush, but this time move it horizontally.

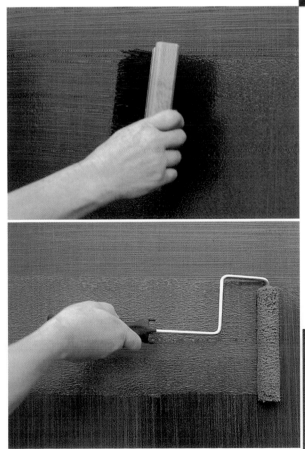

◀ **7.** Apply glaze to the next horizontal band. Again, slightly overlap the area you just glazed.

▼ **8.** The final result.

small-scale combed designs

Like a tile backsplash or a patchwork quilt of individual squares, this project combines small combed sections into an interesting large-scale design.

Because you can draw a grid to keep you on track and will drag for only short distances, you don't need as steady a hand as you do for many other projects that involve dragging.

This project requires a relatively flat surface if you want a look similar to the one shown here. Because the pattern emerges only where the squeegee scrapes away glaze, an underlying texture will prevent

a crisp, neat design. If you comb a design onto a textured surface, glaze will remain in crevices where the blade can't reach.

materials and tools

- Base paint (eggshell sheen)
- Glaze
- Paint or universal colorant to tint glaze
- Level or clip-on laser level
- Colored pencil
- Painter's tape
- Roller with cover
- Paint tray
- Chip brush
- Combing tool or squeegee with a toothed blade (see tip, page 95)
- Cotton T-shirt rags

1. Apply two coats of the base color in an eggshell sheen. Allow each coat to dry as the label recommends.

▶ **2.** With a laser level or a standard level, establish the horizontal and vertical lines of your design. For a pattern like the one shown here, base the dimensions on the size of your combing tool. Mark with a colored pencil matched to the glaze color, not with a standard pencil or a carpenter's chalk line. You will be covering the lines with glaze, which makes them impossible to remove.

▶ **3.** Prepare a medium glaze (see page 29). Apply it with a roller to an area no larger than about 3 by 3 feet.

▶ **4.** Immediately drag the squeegee or other combing tool through the glaze to create a square filled with lines that run one way. Wipe off the blade with a damp cloth. Rotate the tool 90 degrees and drag the next block. Repeat this process until you have combed the entire section. Press with both hands on the tool, if necessary, so that it removes as much glaze as possible from sections where you don't want to see glaze.

▶ **5.** Roll glaze onto the next area and repeat the combing process. Try to just barely overlap the glaze on the line that separates squares so you can comb away any excess while you create the pattern.

tip BEFORE YOU BEGIN, check whether there are any sections of the wall that are too small for your combing tool to fit, such as areas between window trim and a corner. Cut smaller combs for these areas from stiff cardboard, spare squeegee blades, or similar materials.

combed checks

By applying two coats of glaze and combing one vertically and the other horizontally, you can create a variety of checked designs. Use a single color of glaze, as shown here, or select contrasting colors.

Combing through the glaze freehand results in irregularities reminiscent of handwoven cloth. If you'd rather have an underlying grid to guide you, either mark lines with a colored pencil or clip a laser level to the wall. Don't mark with a pencil or a carpenter's chalk line, as glaze will get onto the lines, making them impossible to remove.

If you decide to use two glaze colors, remember that they will create a third where the combed bands intersect, so test first.

materials and tools

- Base paint (eggshell sheen)
- Glaze
- Paint or universal colorant to tint glaze
- Level or clip-on laser level (optional)
- Colored pencil (optional)
- Painter's tape
- Roller with cover
- Paint tray
- Chip brush
- Combing tool or squeegee with a toothed blade
- Smaller combing tool for corners and small spaces
- Painter's 5-in-1 tool or drywall knife
- Cotton T-shirt rags

1. Apply two coats of the base color in an eggshell sheen. Allow each to dry as the label recommends.

2. Apply painter's tape to the top and bottom of the wall. You can also tape the corner where you will begin glazing, but do not tape the far corner, because you will be dragging glaze into that spot. Some of the glaze would inevitably slide under the tape, resulting in a dark blotch.

3. Prepare a medium glaze (see page 29). If you want to make the horizontal stripes first, as shown here, roll the glaze into a band that extends across the wall and is a little more than twice as wide as the length of your dragging tool.

▶ **4.** Immediately go over the area with the dragging tool. Press down hard so you scrape away as much glaze as possible wherever the teeth touch the wall.

◀ **5.** When you near the far corner, lift the tool and switch to a small handmade comb without a handle. This will enable you to reach all the way into the corner and pull any excess glaze onto the adjoining wall. Cut this comb from cardboard (make several) or from a spare squeegee blade.

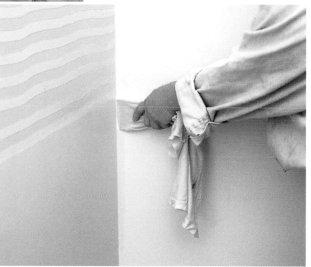

▶ **6.** Immediately wipe off any glaze that you got on the adjoining wall. Use a barely damp cloth wrapped around the blade of a drywall knife or a painter's 5-in-1 tool so you can wipe all the way into the corner without smudging the wall that you have just combed.

7. Repeat steps 3 through 6 for the rest of the wall.

cutting a custom comb

IT'S EASY TO MAKE a custom-sized dragging tool from a squeegee with a rubber blade. Mark teeth on the side of the blade where you can see a rubber reinforcing rib. With a utility knife, cut along the lines as deep as the rib, then cut out the bottom of each opening.

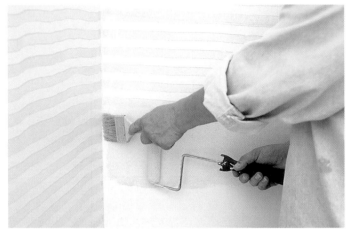

▲ 8. When the glaze on the first wall is thoroughly dry, create the horizontal stripes on the adjoining wall using the same process. To avoid getting too much glaze near corners, stay an inch or two back from the corner when you roll the glaze on. Dab with a chip brush to work some of that glaze into the corner.

▶ 9. When the first layer of glaze is dry, roll on the second layer. Work vertically, with glaze extending from the top of the wall to the bottom, in columns that are a little wider than two lengths of your combing tool.

◀ 10. Comb through the fresh glaze in a single pass from the top of the wall to the bottom. If you have to get off of a ladder or stepstool, hold the squeegee to the wall while you reposition yourself, then keep combing.

▼ 11. The final result.

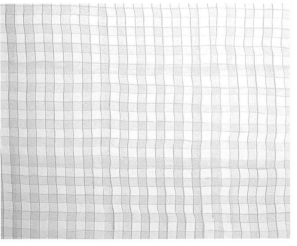

plaid

By using squeegees with different tooth patterns, you can produce plaids. The process is almost the same as for creating checks.

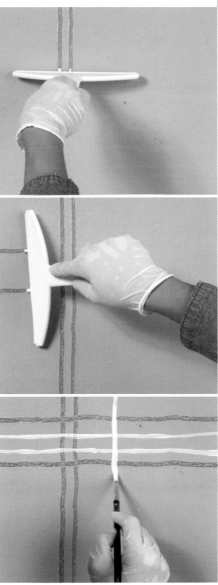

1. Cover the wall with two coats of base paint in an eggshell sheen. When the second coat is dry, snap a reference grid on the wall using a level and a carpenter's chalk line.

▲ **2.** Prepare a medium to opaque glaze (see page 29). Roll the glaze onto a section of the wall about 2 or 3 feet square.

◄ **3.** Using a squeegee that has two teeth close together, drag vertically through the glaze to reveal narrow bands of the base paint. Use the chalk lines that are still visible as a general guide to help you keep straight lines.

◄ **4.** Immediately drag horizontal lines using a squeegee with teeth spaced farther apart. Wipe off the blade with a rag after each pass.

5. Repeat steps 2 through 4. Before each pass, align the squeegee teeth to keep the lines as straight as possible.

◄ **6.** When the glaze is dry, paint accent lines with an artist's brush. Twist the loaded brush as you move it so the paint goes on evenly.

materials and tools

- Base paint (eggshell sheen)
- Glaze
- Paint or universal colorant to tint glaze
- Accent paint
- Carpenter's chalk line
- Level
- Painter's tape
- Roller with cover
- Paint tray
- Chip brush
- Two squeegees cut to make plaid design
- Smaller combing tool for corners and small spaces
- Artist's paintbrush
- Cotton T-shirt rags

rolled squares

Besides using combs and squeegees to create dragged effects, you can also use rollers modified with tape. The resulting squares aren't as precise, but the slight variation looks great and the work goes quickly.

Have extra roller covers and tape on hand in case paint saturates a roller and causes the tape to come loose. Use standard masking tape, not low-tack painter's tape. Also have a small brush handy so you can fill in gaps and make touch-ups. This technique needs to be done on a smooth wall. Fill cracks and indentations and top the filler with primer before you begin.

materials and tools

- Two colors of paint (any sheen)
- 9-inch roller with at least two covers ($\frac{3}{8}$-inch nap; "woven" type)
- Paint tray
- 1-inch brush to clean roller
- Wider brush for edge bands
- Small, flat-tipped paintbrush for touch-ups
- 1-inch-wide masking tape
- Level
- Colored pencil to match the square color
- Cotton T-shirt rags

tip YOU CAN USE THIS technique to create vertical or horizontal stripes, as well as squares. Spacing taped and untaped areas $1\frac{1}{2}$ or 3 inches wide also works well.

1. With a roller, paint the entire wall with the color you want the squares to be. Use a standard roller for these coats.

▲ **2.** While the base paint dries, prepare a fresh roller cover to make the square design. Starting 1 inch from one end, wrap the cover with bands of tape. Place the first band loosely around the roller. Wrap the next piece tightly. Alternate loose and tight areas until you cover the roller. Then remove the loose tape.

▲ **3.** With the level, mark a vertical guideline at one end of the wall. Load the taped roller with the second color of paint. With the 1-inch-wide brush, wipe excess paint off taped sections.

4. Starting at the top of the wall, roll down along the guideline as far as you can without touching the floor with the roller. Repeat this process across the wall. For each new set of lines, maintain even spacing by painting one line that overlaps the previous one.

◄ **5.** Paint the horizontal lines as you did the vertical ones. The vertical stripes need not dry first.

6. Use a damp rag to clean up any smudged areas. Then extend the design into spaces too small for the roller to fit. Don't be obsessive about creating perfect squares, however; variation is part of the charm of this effect. When the paint is dry to the touch, draw a line near the floor and paint a faux baseboard. You can also paint faux trim around windows and doors and faux crown molding next to the ceiling. The faux molding covers up edge areas where the roller didn't reach (see page 49).

CHOOSING COLORS
for dragged effects

The technique you choose determines how much contrast you'll want in the base and glaze colors. Strié and linen work best when the base and glaze are close on the color wheel but one is light in value and the other is dark, so you see the overall effect as one color. Combing works with subtle or distinct combinations.

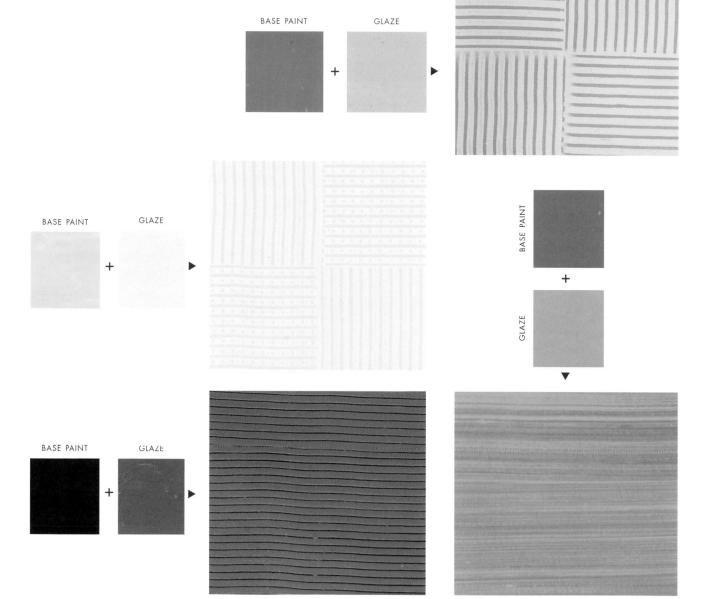

BASE PAINT + GLAZE ▶

BASE PAINT + GLAZE ▶

BASE PAINT + GLAZE ▶

BASE PAINT + GLAZE ▼

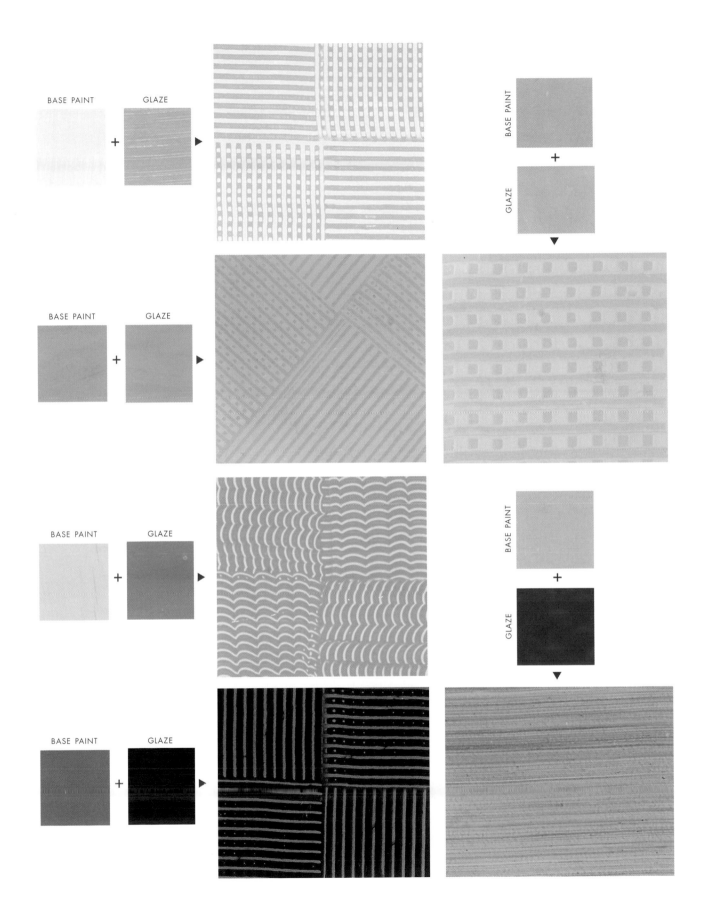

BASE PAINT   GLAZE

BASE PAINT

+

GLAZE

BASE PAINT   GLAZE

BASE PAINT   GLAZE

BASE PAINT

+

GLAZE

BASE PAINT   GLAZE

stencils

Stencils allow people with modest artistic talent to create a wide range of decorative effects. There are many styles of stencils, including elaborate shapes and those that emphasize specific historical periods. Small stencils in a single row look great running along the top of a wall, while repeating, large-format stencils create designs that look almost like wallpaper.

Once you settle on a specific stencil, there are still many ways to use it. You can paint the stencil a single color or use different colors for specific parts of the design. And if you stencil with venetian plaster or another textured material rather than standard paint, your design can have a three-dimensional quality.

▶ A simple single-color stencil suits the early American look of this kitchen. Repeated over the wainscot and along the top of the walls, the painted design works well as a substitute for a chair rail and crown molding.

▼ With letter stencil, write your child's name or your favorite quote over a mottled background.

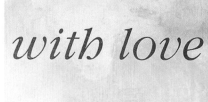

with love

◄ Traditional border stencils and stand-alone designs decorate the walls of this historic house. The stencils as well as the basic wall and trim paint are all historically accurate colors that reflect the earth pigments used to color early paints.

▼ Lightly sanded, the stenciled and sponge-painted decorations on this wall take on the soft elegance of a fine, well-worn antique.

◄ With an overlay stencil, you can create designs similar to those on the top panels of these doors. This type of stencil comes in layers, with the base stencil establishing the basic pattern. Overlay stencils guide you in adding shading or features that lie on top of other elements.

floor and ceiling stencils

Floors and ceilings are often overlooked as decorative elements, yet they are great places to use stenciled designs. On a floor, stenciling can frame specific areas, much as area rugs do. Floor stencils also dress up plain surfaces or add enough interest to worn surfaces so that you notice the decoration and not the scratches. On a ceiling, stencils can define areas of a room, which helps make them feel cozier. They can also add to or subtract from the apparent height of a room.

▶ Painted leaves add a touch of finery to a well-worn floor but they still fit with the faded-glory look of the old house.

▼ When a border stencil coordinates with other decorative elements in a room, it makes the floor seem like part of the room's décor. The decision to use a simple design in a muted color keeps it from seeming overly cute.

▼ A network of molding strips plus painted designs mimics the look of a traditional coffered ceiling. True coffered ceilings help with the acoustics in a room, which can't be said of faux versions. However, painted designs do fulfill another purpose of true coffered ceilings: visually lowering the surface so that the space underneath seems cozier. The designs shown here were painted by hand, but similar ones could be done with stencils.

▲ Painted in a wood tone on a hardwood floor, stenciled designs take on the look of expensive inlays. Some artists favor semitransparent oils for this technique because these paints allow some of the wood grain to show through. The oils stick to most floor finishes and can then be coated with clear polyurethane or another floor finish so the design doesn't wear off.

▲ Like the ornate ceiling medallions popular from the 18th to the 20th century, a painted design on a ceiling draws attention to what goes on underneath. The effect is particularly useful centered over a dining table. Designs similar to this can be painted by hand or stenciled in.

◄ When rooms are tucked into the eaves of a roof, it's never clear whether the sloping section is part of the wall or part of the ceiling. Here, the stenciled design makes it clear that the wall extends all the way up to the flat portion of the ceiling. This makes the room seem taller and more spacious.

stenciled border

With a single stencil and some artist's acrylics, you can add architectural interest to a plain room. Painting a row of repeating designs is often more effective than scattering stencils around the room, especially if you place the row where wood molding might otherwise be. To speed your work, use a stencil that includes several repeats of the design, if possible.

One-layer stencils, as used here, can be painted in a single color or several. If you choose multiple colors, test the effect on a sample board before you begin stenciling your wall. Because you need no glaze for this project, any type of base paint is acceptable, and you can skip a protective finish.

materials and tools

- ◆ Artist's acrylics in various colors
- ◆ Stencil
- ◆ Stencil brushes
- ◆ Waterproof container to use as a palette
- ◆ Painter's tape or spray-on stencil adhesive
- ◆ Level
- ◆ Cotton T-shirt rags

1. Assuming the wall paint is in good condition and you like the color, begin by inspecting the stencil to determine which side goes out. Mark it with a short piece of painter's tape.

▶ **2.** Apply painter's tape to one edge of the stencil, or spray the back with stencil adhesive. Wait for the adhesive to become tacky, if you are using it. Using a level, position the stencil where you want the design.

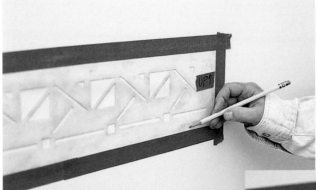

3. With a pencil, mark the spots provided on the stencil to ensure that pattern repeats line up properly. You'll use these dots when you reposition the stencil.

4. Pour a small amount of each color of paint onto a shallow container that's easy to carry. A plastic plate works well. Also gather stencil brushes, which have thick tufts of short, stubby bristles.

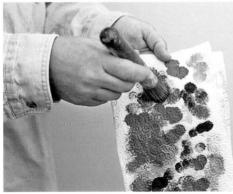

5. Lightly dab a brush into the paint so that the bristles pick up only a little. Blot off any excess on a paper towel. Once you start with a color, paint all sections that need it before you clean the brush and go on to another color. Or use a different brush for each color and wipe the bristles on a dry cloth each time you finish using it.

6. In small, squat openings, transfer the paint with a flicking motion, not with a long brushstroke. This and the other motions used for stenciling are designed to fill openings with color in a way that prevents drips and blobs (see page 108).

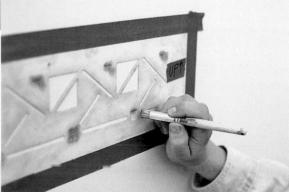

7. Fill in long, thin openings with more of a pouncing motion, as if you were stippling the design.

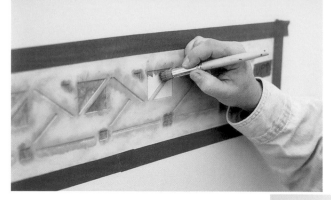

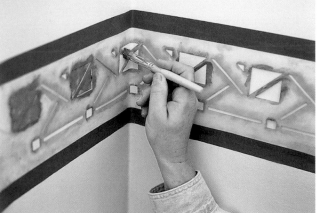

▲ **8.** On wide openings, paint in a circular motion. Work from the edges toward the center so paint doesn't leak under the stencil.

9. When the entire design is painted, pull off the stencil and reposition it once the first section dries. Use the pencil marks you made in step 3, but also check the alignment with a level. Move the stencil slightly, if necessary, to keep it level. Otherwise, slight irregularities will add up and the final stencil will be noticeably out of line with the first one.

▲**10.** As you near a corner, be aware that the stencil may not end where the wall does. You may be able to bend a simple stencil like this into the corner and continue with the design on the next wall. Another option is to stretch out or condense the design so that it fits. You may be able to add slightly more space between elements, for example.

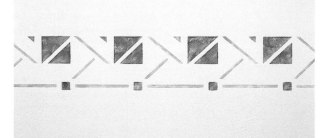

◀**11.** The final result.

stencil strokes

PAINTING USING A STENCIL REQUIRES different brushstrokes than you usually use to paint a wall. Brushing back and forth would force paint underneath the stencil, ruining the crisp shapes you are trying to create. Try these techniques instead.

Move the brush in circles.

Dab the brush in and out, as if you were stippling.

Flick the brush up and down.

raised stencil

A skillful painter can create the illusion of texture by adding shadow lines in all the right places. But with a raised stencil, you don't have to pretend. The design is naturally three-dimensional.

Creating a raised stencil design is almost as easy as painting a standard one. You simply spread drywall joint compound, venetian plaster, or another texture material into the stencil's openings rather than brush paint over them. Texture materials take longer to dry, however, so be especially careful not to create smudges as you reposition the stencil. You may want to mark where the stencil will be across the entire wall before you begin. Then you can stencil every other section and wait for those to dry before filling intervening areas.

This project was created with standard joint compound and metallic paints, but you could use other materials. Raised stencils can go over any type of paint that is in good condition.

materials and tools

- Stencil
- Painter's tape or spray-on stencil adhesive
- Level
- Pencil
- Joint compound or other texture material
- 2- or 3-inch flexible drywall knife
- 6-inch drywall knife (stiff or flexible)
- Small spatula
- Metallic paint or other paint for stencil areas
- Chisel-tip artist's brush
- Cotton T-shirt rags

1. Check the stencil to see which side goes out. If you are using spray adhesive, coat the back of the stencil with it and wait for the adhesive to become tacky. If you are using painter's tape, smooth it along one edge of the stencil.

◄ **2.** Position the stencil on the wall. Check the alignment with a level before you firmly press it into place or finish taping it down. With a pencil, mark the spots provided on the stencil to ensure that pattern repeats line up properly.

▲ **3.** With the narrower drywall knife, fill the openings with a thin layer of drywall mud or other texture material. Remove any excess and scrape it onto the other drywall knife. Use the larger knife as a plasterer's hawk to keep the material handy until you need it for the next stencil area.

◄ **4.** Remove the stencil as soon as you complete the area. If there are smudges, tidy up the design with a small spatula.

tip TO SECURE THE STENCIL to the wall, use either painter's tape or spray-on stencil adhesive. The adhesive is easier to use because it holds the stencil flatter to the wall, reducing the chance of texture material getting under the stencil.

5. When the first area is dry, carefully reposition the stencil so you can repeat steps 3 and 4. Use the marks on the stencil as a guide, but check the alignment with a level if the design needs to be perfectly level or horizontal.

6. When all of the texture material is dry, paint the design with a chisel-tip artist's brush.

a shortcut

INSTEAD OF PAINTING a raised stencil design, you can leave the texture material just as it is. Joint compound dries to a slightly off-white color. If you use venetian plaster or the sculpture-effects products made by some decorative paint manufacturers, you can incorporate color into the material before you apply it to the wall. This approach creates sections with uniform color, without the brushstrokes and blended colors possible when you paint the design.

PLASTER
effects

Plaster effects emphasize the texture of a wall. It once took a lot of training to create these looks, because the materials were tricky, containing things such as cement-based stucco and true venetian plaster made from lime putty and marble dust. Today, with acrylic variations, you can create anything from a sandy surface with brush or trowel marks to the polished look of venetian plaster.

▲ A technique known as skip troweling produces a texture like this. First a coat of joint compound or other texture material is spread over the entire surface. For the second coat, material is dabbed on sparingly so that when it's smoothed over with a trowel, some of the initial coat is still exposed.

▶ The soft, subdued texture of tone-on-tone venetian plaster helps create a serene mood in a bedroom.

◄ By adapting the stripes project shown on pages 72–74, you can use venetian plaster to create a softly textured design like this.

▼ A heavily textured surface requires two coats of coarse-textured material, such as plaster made with relatively large grains of sand. The initial coat covers the entire surface. The second coat is dabbed on and lightly troweled in random directions.

▲ With just a single color of venetian plaster, you can create beautiful tone-on-tone effects. The more layers you apply, the richer the texture, as each layer winds up with a slightly different amount of polishing.

► Texture materials can be used to create surfaces that closely resemble stone or brick. Just as in the painted limestone blocks project shown on pages 75–77, the mortar joints are easy to create with masking tape that's removed once the rest of the finish is in place.

polished venetian plaster

Silky smooth polished venetian plaster is one of the most elegant finishes you can put on a wall. Because you create the gloss by rubbing the surface vigorously with a steel trowel, the look is distinctly different from the shine of a glossy polyurethane or shellac coating. Instead of being shiny all over, the gloss level seems to undulate and shift as you walk by.

True venetian plaster, made with lime putty and marble dust, needs to be polished almost immediately after it is troweled onto a surface. Acrylic products are more forgiving. Formulas vary by manufacturer, so read the label for guidance on when to begin polishing. In general, the sooner you start, the higher gloss you can achieve. But an early start increases the risk of accidentally digging into the surface and scraping off some of the plaster.

Check the label to be sure you have prepared the wall properly for venetian plaster. Many products must be applied over flat paint or primer.

materials and tools

- Venetian plaster tinted at the paint store
- Steel spatula or 6-inch drywall knife with rounded corners
- Another 6-inch drywall knife to use as a hawk
- 400- and 600-grit sandpaper
- Cotton T-shirt rags

tip IF BITS OF PLASTER begin to dry on your application tool, wipe it clean with a damp cloth. Plaster that cakes on the spatula or drywall knife will scratch the surface you are decorating.

2. Prepare a steel spatula or a wide drywall knife to be your application tool. Sand off sharp corners and any burrs along the blade.

1. Prepare the wall as specified on the venetian plaster label. This often means coating existing paint with PVA primer, the same type you'd use on new drywall.

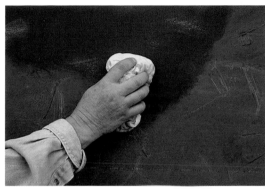

3. Working in an area no more than 3 by 3 feet, spread a thin coat of the plaster by making a series of overlapping X's. Smooth over any ridges to leave the surface as flat as possible. Scrape excess plaster onto another drywall knife and use this material to reload your application tool for the next section.

4. When the first coat is dry, perhaps in one to four hours, lightly sand the surface with 400-grit sandpaper. Wipe off the sanding dust with a damp rag.

5. Apply a second coat of plaster using the same technique. Remove any ridges by going over the area again in a different direction.

6. Once dry, sand the second coat with 600-grit sandpaper to remove high spots. Though some venetian plaster products can be polished when they are only partially dry, you're less likely to gouge the surface if you allow the material to dry fully. Wipe off the dust with a damp rag.

7. Finally, polish the plaster. Hold your application tool almost flat against the wall. Press down on the blade and rub it in a crisscross motion to burnish the plaster. Be careful not to nick the surface. If you do, patch it with a little leftover plaster, wait the recommended time, and polish the area again.

muticolored venetian plaster

By overlapping and partially blending several colors of
venetian plaster, you can create complex designs reminiscent
of paintings created with stiff paint and a spatula.

The three colors used here provide
considerable contrast, but the
technique could also be done with
different tints of a single color. Apply
each color to a separate section of
the wall, then slightly blend by
rubbing over them with your
application tool. Remember that
mixing colors that are opposite each
other on the color wheel results in
gray. So the more contrast in the
colors you select, the less you should
blend them on the wall if you don't
want to make the colors muddy.
Use a light touch.

This project uses acrylic venetian
plaster. Products vary by manufacturer,
so be sure to read the label and
prepare the surface properly.

Though the finish looks complex,
it's easier to create than a single-
color, polished one. You don't have
to sand or smooth the plaster, just
trowel it on. But because the pattern
is random, you'll need to step back
occasionally to make sure the overall
effect stays consistent.

materials and tools

- Venetian plaster in three colors
- Steel spatula or 6-inch drywall
  knife with rounded corners
- Cotton T-shirt rags
- Disposable gloves

1. Prepare the wall as specified on the venetian plaster label, often by coating existing paint with PVA primer.

▲ **2.** Using a steel spatula or a wide drywall knife that has been sanded to remove sharp corners and burrs (see page 115), spread one color of the plaster over scattered sections of the wall.

▲ **3.** Coat some of the bare areas with plaster in a different color.

◄ **4.** Fill in remaining areas with the third color.

▶ **5.** With the spatula or drywall knife, go over parts of the plaster to blend the colors somewhat. If you want a vertical design, move the tool primarily up and down. Flatten thick areas, which are likely to crack as they dry, but don't attempt to create a uniformly smooth surface.

◄ **6.** When you get to a corner, use your application tool to pull excess material onto the adjoining wall.

▼ **7.** Use your gloved hand to smooth material into the corner.

8. Repeat steps 2 through 7 for the rest of the wall.

◄ **9.** The final result.

stenciled venetian plaster

Adding a raised stencil design to a two-tone venetian plaster background results in an intriguing finish with patterns that seem to fade away in some sections but stand proud in others.

Because there's a lot going on, stick with a single color for the plaster but select two tints, one a little lighter than the other. For the stenciled areas, use whichever tint you choose for the second coat if you want the stencil to blend into the background. For an all-over design similar to the one shown here, select a large-format stencil with several repeats.

Once the plaster is dry, rub an umber glaze over the surface. The glaze tones down the contrast in the base colors, adds highlights to the stenciled design, and magically pulls all the elements together. Start with a medium glaze and allow it to dry.

If you want a darker color, you can always apply a second coat later.

As with all venetian plaster projects, be sure to read the label to find out how to prepare the wall. You may need to paint it first with a PVA primer.

materials and tools

- ◆ Venetian plaster in two colors
- ◆ Umber glaze, or classic glaze plus umber paint
- ◆ Protective finish (optional)
- ◆ Flat stainless-steel trowel, steel spatula, or flexible 6-inch drywall knife
- ◆ 3-inch steel spatula or flexible drywall knife
- ◆ Additional trowel or drywall knife to use as a hawk
- ◆ Disposable gloves
- ◆ 400-grit sandpaper
- ◆ Stencil
- ◆ Painter's tape or stencil adhesive
- ◆ Level
- ◆ Pencil
- ◆ 4-inch chip brush or other glaze application tool
- ◆ Cotton T-shirt rags

1. Prepare the wall as specified on the venetian plaster label.

▲ **2.** Using a flat stainless-steel trowel or a wide spatula or drywall knife with sanded corners (see page 115), spread a thin layer of the base color over the wall. Don't worry if you skip a few areas or leave thin sections.

3. When the first layer is dry, lightly sand the surface with a folded piece of 400-grit sandpaper. Wipe off the dust with a damp rag.

▲ **4.** Apply the second color in patches. Trowel the material smooth, but leave some areas where the base coat still shows.

▶ **5.** When the second coat is dry, sand it with 400-grit sandpaper. Wipe away the dust with a damp rag.

◀ **6.** Inspect the stencil to see which side goes out. Spray the back with stencil adhesive and wait for it to become tacky, or smooth painter's tape along one edge of the stencil. (Adhesive works better than tape for this project.) Position the stencil at the top of the wall in a location that's not too noticeable, such as where you enter the room.

▶ **7.** With a pencil, mark the spots provided on the stencil to ensure that pattern repeats line up properly.

◄ 8. With the narrower spatula or drywall knife, spread a thin layer of plaster over the stencil openings. Use the tool like a squeegee, but avoid putting so much pressure on it that you cause the stencil to buckle or lift.

9. Immediately remove the stencil. Wipe off any excess plaster. Reposition the stencil with the pencil marks you made in step 7 as a guide, but check the placement with a level. Shift the stencil slightly, if necessary, so the design doesn't slant.

▲ 10. Once all the stenciling is done and the plaster is dry, brush an umber glaze over the surface. A medium formula (see page 29) works well. Add more paint if you want a darker glaze.

▲ 11. With a cotton rag, rub the glaze to distribute it over the surface and work it into the edges of the stencil design.

▶ 12. The final result.

embossed textures

By pressing burlap or another coarsely woven fabric into damp venetian plaster, you can create a rich embossed design. While you might be tempted to strive for a uniform texture throughout a room, you'll have a much easier time, and probably better results, if you emboss only random areas. This way, you don't have to worry about smoothing the fabric into straight lines where sections meet.

If you want a bit of base color to peek through, either apply a thin first coat of venetian plaster in a base color, or paint the wall that color (the approach shown here). In either case, avoid covering the entire surface when you apply venetian plaster for the embossing step.

To emboss the design, simply press burlap into the plaster, then peel back the fabric. You should be able to reposition it several times before the weave becomes clogged with plaster. When that happens, rinse off the burlap in a bucket of water and let the cloth dry. Pick up a dry piece and continue to extend the texture across the wall.

materials and tools

- ◆ Base paint (flat)
- ◆ Venetian plaster
- ◆ At least one piece of burlap cut to an irregular shape
- ◆ Roller and cover
- ◆ Roller tray
- ◆ Disposable gloves
- ◆ Flat stainless-steel trowel or flexible 6-inch drywall knife with rounded corners
- ◆ Wash bucket
- ◆ Cotton T-shirt rag

1. Prepare the wall as recommended on the venetian plaster label. After priming, if necessary, roll base paint over the wall.

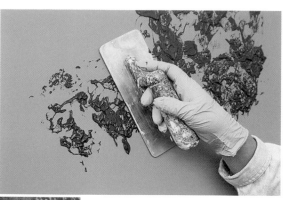

▲**2.** Dab blobs of venetian plaster onto the wall and trowel over them to cover up most but not all of the base paint.

◄**3.** Press burlap into the plaster and smooth it over with the trowel or drywall knife. Immediately peel off the burlap.

4. Go on to adjoining areas. Reuse the burlap as long as it still creates a similar texture. If it picks up too much plaster, switch to a clean, dry piece. Burlap can be reused after being rinsed in clean water and hung to dry.

◄**5.** When the plaster is dry, apply a sealer such as shellac or clear acrylic. A shiny sealer accentuates the texture.

▼**6.** The final result.

lace designs

Besides embossing venetian plaster with plain fabric, you can use lace like a stencil to create a design. Create a base coat first with paint or a thin layer of plaster. Then, working in one section at a time, trowel plaster through the lace.

If you apply the lace and plaster in random areas, covering slightly different sections of the lace each time, you don't have to worry about lining anything up. For a more formal look, however, you could use an entire lace panel to create textured blocks across a wall.

materials and tools

- Base paint in flat sheen (optional)
- Roller and cover (optional)
- Roller tray (optional)
- Venetian plaster
- Lace curtain (scrap or full panel)
- Disposable gloves
- Flat stainless-steel trowel or flexible 6-inch drywall knife with rounded corners (see page 115)
- Wash bucket
- Cotton T-shirt rags

1. Prepare the wall as recommended on the venetian plaster label. After priming, if it is necessary, roll base paint over the wall or trowel on a thin layer of plaster.

◀ **2.** When the first coat is dry, position the lace. Dab a little plaster through the lace to hold the piece in place.

◀ **3.** With the trowel or drywall knife, coat as much of the lace as you wish with plaster. Use the tool like a squeegee to smooth the plaster and remove the excess. The plaster should be thin, about even with the top of the lace.

◀ **4.** Peel back the lace and reposition it. Repeat steps 2 and 3, but vary which section of lace you use to transfer the design so that you wind up with an irregular look, not a definite repeating pattern.

5. If the lace becomes clogged with plaster, rinse it in a bucket of water. Wring out excess water before you resume using the lace, or use a clean, dry piece.

◀ **6.** The final effect.

plaster with mix-ins

Just as you can transform plain ice cream by mixing in candy or nuts, you can create magical effects by embellishing plaster-type materials with birdseed, bits of straw, or other small, lightweight ingredients.

This project incorporates Niger thistle, a type of birdseed sold for feeding to finches, in a skim coating of drywall mud. The finish can be left its natural color or tinted with glaze once the material has dried.

You can apply this finish over new drywall or existing paint. Wash old paint first if it is greasy or spattered with soap. Be sure to buy standard drywall mud, also known as joint compound. Don't use spackle, quick-setting joint compound, or lightweight joint compound.

materials and tools

- Drywall mud
- Niger thistle birdseed
- Mixing container and paddle
- Flat trowel or drywall knife with rounded corners (see page 115)
- Sponge float
- Disposable gloves
- Glaze tinted with paint or universal colorant (optional)
- Wide, thick brush
- Clear acrylic or other sealer

► **1.** Combine measured amounts of birdseed and drywall mud in a mixing container and stir until the consistency is creamy. Keep track of the proportions so you can prepare an identical batch if you run short. For each quart of drywall mud, you will need just a few tablespoons of birdseed.

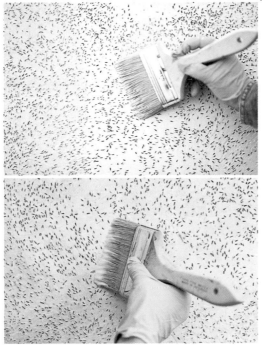

2. Trowel the mixture onto the wall. Aim for a fairly flat surface, but don't worry if you see some trowel marks. Allow the coating to dry thoroughly, typically 24 to 48 hours.

3. Go over the surface with a damp sponge float (typically sold for smoothing grout between tiles). The float will remove the surface skim of drywall mud, exposing the birdseed. Rub only enough to expose the seeds, as you don't want to make them fall out. Rinse the sponge frequently.

4. Allow the surface to dry. The tiny black seeds look great with the unadorned, off-white color of the drywall mud. Proceed to step 6 if you want to keep this look.

5. If you want to tint the drywall mud, prepare an opaque or medium glaze (see page 29). Brush it onto the wall, as if you were mottling with a brush (see page 62). Allow the glaze to dry.

6. Brush on a clear sealer. Although a sealer is optional with many decorative paint techniques, it is essential with this one because it helps keep the seeds in place.

embedding straw

YOU CAN ALSO ADD TEXTURE with wheat straw. Follow the same basic procedure as with birdseed, but skip the step involving a sponge float. Instead, if you want to see bits of exposed straw in the finish, press additional straw into the mixture of straw and drywall mud just after you trowel it onto the wall. Plaster over these strands only partially.

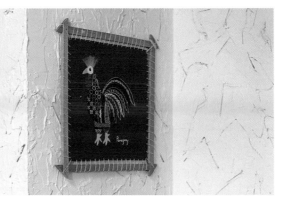

special
EFFECTS

Wood graining, glow-in-the-dark designs, frottage, marbling, clouds—the special effects that can be created with ordinary and specialty paints are almost endless. Some are suitable for walls, while others, such as marbling and wood graining, are more likely to show up on other surfaces, such as woodwork or furniture.

▲ Thin plastic, used in a technique called frottage, produces a sumptuous texture in paint that resembles polished leather. The painter rolls on the finish, presses the plastic onto the paint while it is still wet, and then pulls off the covering, leaving the interesting pattern behind. Glaze adds color and brings out the texture.

▶ Frottage was also used in this room, except that the painter worked with big drifts of lightweight plastic and used a hairdryer to push its drape-like folds into the paint.

◀ It takes an experienced faux painter—or a skilled woodworker—to create curved paneling that truly looks like wood. But fantasy wood is easier to render because the design doesn't have to be so subtle. Fantasy finishes borrow from traditional faux techniques but substitute wild colors or exaggerated features. Their purpose is not to fool but to entertain.

▼ Clouds painted with the purples and yellows of sunset give way to night as they cross the barrel ceiling of this bedroom. The twinkling stars are tiny lights.

◀ Marbling, gilding, a little stenciling, and even a few clouds dress up this bathroom, but the effect isn't overwhelming, as the painter used cool colors in muted shades.

clouds

Clouds are one of the most popular special effects you can create with paint. There are as many methods as there are types of clouds, but whichever approach you take, it's hard to go wrong.

If you want to mimic a specific type of cloud, be sure to practice beforehand. Painting realistic clouds usually involves mottling, and it's difficult to know when to stop. If you blend too much, you'll wind up with fog.

materials and tools

- ◆ Base paint (eggshell sheen)
- ◆ Glaze
- ◆ Paint or universal colorants to tint glaze
- ◆ Small roller with cover
- ◆ 3-inch chip brush
- ◆ Cheesecloth or cotton T-shirt rags
- ◆ Sea-wool sponge (if desired)
- ◆ Disposable gloves

1. Apply two coats of the base paint, which is typically blue. Allow each to dry as the label recommends.

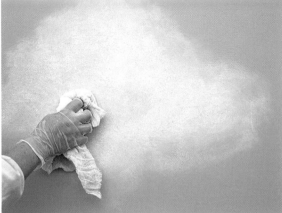

▲**2.** When the final base coat is dry, prepare a medium to opaque glaze (see page 29) tinted white. Roll it onto the wall over an area where you want to center the main part of a cloud. Keep ragged edges and don't apply the glaze to an area larger than 3 by 3 feet.

▲**3.** With a gloved hand, repeatedly dab a cheese-cloth pouf (see page 61) or a cotton T-shirt rag into the glaze and out onto the surrounding paint. Leave some areas more opaque than others.

▲**4.** Add depth and drama by streaking dark blue or gray glaze along the bottom of the cloud. With cheesecloth or a rag, slightly blend the color with the surrounding glaze.

◄**5.** If you want wisps of the cloud to trail out behind, brush on a few lines of white glaze. Blend this too.

tip IF YOU DECIDE TO paint clouds on a ceiling, consider extending the design, or at least the base color, partway down the walls to mimic how the sky looks outdoors. To mark the base of the sky, you might want to add a strip of molding that's even with the top of the room's door and window trim.

wood graining

Many people consider wood graining the ultimate form of decorative or faux painting. Others cringe at the notion of using paint instead of the real thing. Whichever side you're on, there are times when a little bit of wood graining might be just what's needed to mask a metal insert in paneling or to dress up a flea market find.

You can use a variety of techniques, depending on the type of wood you are trying to mimic and the way individual boards were sawn from the log. If you want the look of vertical-grain fir, for example, strié techniques work well (see pages 88–89). If you want the vivid flame-shaped patterns seen on flat-sawn boards with alternating bands of dark and light wood, such as long leaf pine, try the veining technique used in marbling (see pages 139–141).

This project creates the look of curly maple, also known as fiddle-back because the wood is often used in stringed instruments. In an actual board, the wood fibers undulate in and out rather than lie flat. The undulations affect the way light reflects off the surface, producing the curly look. The wood is actually all one color. Created with glaze, however, a fiddleback design requires glaze several shades darker than the base paint.

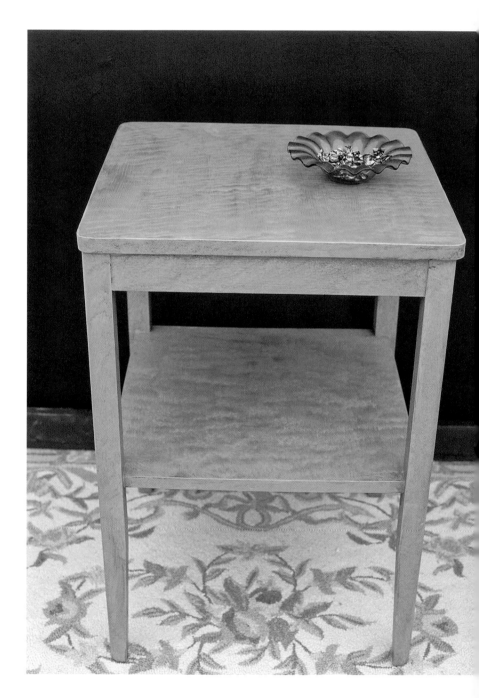

materials and tools

- Tan base paint (eggshell sheen)
- Brush or roller to apply base paint
- Glaze
- Brown paint or universal colorant to tint glaze
- Chip brush
- Wood-graining brush or other long-bristle brush 1½ to 2 inches wide
- Softening brush or other thick brush with soft bristles
- Disposable gloves
- Cotton T-shirt rags

1. Patch any holes and prime the surface, if necessary. Over that, apply two coats of the base color in an eggshell sheen.

▲ **2.** When the final base coat is dry, prepare a medium glaze (see page 29). With the chip brush, apply the glaze to the surface in parallel strokes. Don't worry about making the glaze look even. If your project is larger than about 2 square feet, work in sections.

▲ **3.** Pick up the graining brush and hold it as shown, with a couple of your fingers on the bristles so they splay out. Push down into the glaze and go forward (away from you) half an inch or so to produce the curly design. Work in rows, but make them irregular rather than perfectly vertical.

4. Wipe the bristles on a clean, dry rag periodically so they don't become clogged with glaze.

▲ **5.** When you have created the grain over the area, use the softening brush to blend the design. Brush very lightly across the surface, then lengthwise.

spattering

Spattering is a technique that creates a random pattern of dots on a painted surface. The dots can be tiny and scattered, as they are on the table being painted here, or larger and so closely packed that the surface resembles granite.

The key to creating a successful spattering project is to practice first on old newspapers or scrap cardboard. There are many variables, and the combination you select will determine how your project turns out. For example, your spattering brush needs to have thick, fairly stiff bristles, but it can range from an old toothbrush to an expensive pouncer, the tool used for this project. You can use the paint straight or dilute it slightly by spritzing the brush with alcohol before you dip the bristles in the finish. You can hold the brush different distances from the surface, and you can flick off paint droplets in various ways.

Once you've arrived at a specific technique that you like, practice it again from start to finish to make sure you can repeat it. Then tackle your actual project. You'll probably be done quickly, since spattering is a quick and easy project.

materials and tools

- Base paint (any sheen)
- Spatter paint (small amounts are usually enough)
- Denatured alcohol
- Spray bottle
- Plastic plates or other shallow containers
- Spatter brush, such as a pouncer
- Disposable gloves
- Cotton T-shirt rags

1. Over a properly prepared surface, paint two coats of the base color. Any sheen is fine.

▶ **2.** Pour denatured alcohol into a labeled spray bottle. Spritz alcohol onto the tips of the bristles in your spattering brush.

◀ **3.** Pour a little of the first spatter color onto a plastic plate or other shallow container. Lightly dip just the bristle tips of your spattering brush into the paint.

▶ **4.** With a gloved finger or a chopstick or other small stick, flick paint off the brush and onto the surface you are decorating. Pull the paint off towards you, rather than directing it out, away from your body. Repeat until there are as many dots as you wish.

5. When you have applied enough of the first color, repeat steps 2–4 with each of the other colors.

◀ **6.** If paint drips off the brush onto the surface you are decorating, blot the drips up with a cotton cloth wrapped over a finger. Dab in and out, rather than rub, so you are less likely to mar surrounding paint.

frottage

Pressing film or fabric into glaze and then peeling it off produces a finish known as frottage, which is French for "rub." The technique results in a richly varied texture far different from what you can do with a brush or roller.

Materials used to create the texture are limited only by your imagination. Thin plastic, such as dry-cleaner bags or inexpensive drop cloths, work well. You can also experiment with fabric, as shown in the plaster techniques involving burlap (see pages 121–122) or lace (see page 123). Glossy newspaper pages, as used here, transfer some of their ink to the glaze, adding to the mysterious, mottled look. For this effect, use pages from a Sunday magazine or advertising inserts. The ink transfer is subtle, so you won't find whole words or identifiable images appearing in reverse on your wall.

materials and tools

- Base paint (eggshell sheen)
- Painter's tape
- Glaze
- Paints or pigments to tint the glaze
- Rollers with covers (one per glaze color)
- Paint trays (one per color)
- Glossy newspaper pages
- Clear finish, such as acrylic or shellac
- Brush or roller for clear sealer
- Disposable gloves

1. Over a properly prepared surface, apply two coats of base paint. Allow each coat to dry as the label recommends.

2. Apply painter's tape to the top and bottom of the wall. You don't need to tape corners if you will use this technique on adjoining walls.

▲**3.** Crumple sheets of newspaper and open them up. Let the wrinkles set while you prepare several colors of opaque glaze (see page 29). Using separate rollers, apply the glazes in randomly sized blocks over an area about 3 by 3 feet. The blocks should touch each other.

▲**4.** Working quickly, press the pre-wrinkled sheets into the glaze.

▶**5.** As soon as you have pressed paper into all of the glaze in the section you are working on, lift a corner of the first sheet to see whether the ink color has transferred. If it hasn't, leave the paper in place a little longer, then remove it. But don't wait so long that the glaze dries. The room's temperature and the proportion of paint to glaze will affect timing.

◀**6.** If small parts of newspaper stick to the glaze, leave them to add to the look, but brush or roll on a clear finish to seal the surface and keep the bits of paper from falling off. As with all techniques created with glaze, you should also apply sealer if you will need to clean the wall frequently.

tissue paper texture

From burnished gold to hand-rubbed leather, amazing finishes result from manipulating tissue paper and wallpaper paste on a wall. You can use these materials simply to create an interesting texture that gives walls an organic, handmade look. Or, by choosing colors carefully, you can create faux effects.

For the look of gold leaf, paint the textured surface gold, then rub it with a reddish glaze. For leather, choose paint that's reddish brown, brown, or tan and use a darker glaze.

If you aren't aiming for a faux look but simply want a beautifully textured wall, you can stop after you paint the surface or you can top it with a glaze that brings out the texture. In this case, use glaze two shades darker than the paint.

materials and tools

- Wallpaper paste
- Primer, if necessary
- Tissue paper (enough to cover walls, plus extra)
- Paint (eggshell sheen)
- Glaze, if desired
- Pigment or paint to tint glaze
- Chip brushes (1 large, 1 small)
- One or more rollers or brushes (for primer, paste, paint, and glaze)
- Paint tray
- Cotton T-shirt rags
- Disposable gloves

1. Read the label on the wallpaper paste. If necessary, prime the walls.

▶ **2.** Tear edges off the tissue paper. Prepare enough sheets to cover the wall in one layer, plus a few extra sheets.

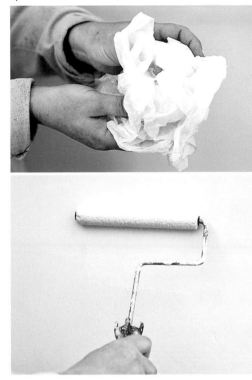

◀ **3.** Crumple the sheets of tissue paper, then open them up.

◀ **4.** Apply wallpaper adhesive to the wall with a roller or a brush. Make sure there are no lumps or bare spots.

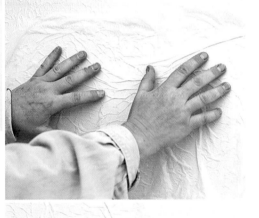

▶ **5.** Position a sheet of paper on the wall and press it into place. Keep the tissue as flat as possible, but don't worry if there are wrinkles.

▶ **6.** With a small chip brush, smooth out some of the wrinkles and manipulate the remaining ones into folds that are securely anchored in the wallpaper paste.

▼ **7.** Apply another sheet to an adjoining section of the wall. Overlap the edge of the first sheet. Use the chip brush to smooth out the tissue or force it into sharp folds. Then tear off the overlapping tissue.

8. If you tear off too much in step 7, or if you neglect to cover small areas with tissue, patch the surface with small pieces. If there isn't enough wallpaper paste on the wall, brush on a little more.

9. Once the paste is dry, apply primer with a roller or a brush. Step back frequently and look for drips, which tend to collect in the creases of the tissue. Use a chip brush to smooth the drips while they are still fluid.

10. When the primer is dry, apply paint in the color of your choice. Again, watch for drips and brush them out of the creases.

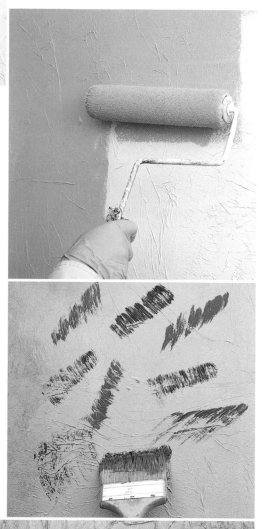

11. After the paint is dry, add glaze if you wish to emphasize the tissue texture. Apply a medium glaze (see page 29) sparingly with the wide chip brush. With a cotton rag or a cheesecloth pouf, distribute the glaze across the surface and work it into the edges of the creases. Use a light touch so you don't tear the tissue.

12. The final result.

marbling

Duplicating the look of marble with paint and glaze is surprisingly easy. Because of the inherent variability of marble, it's hard to go wrong as long as you're careful not to blend the colors so much that they all become one.

Marble consists mostly of calcite, a white mineral. Small amounts of other minerals result in the swirls, bands, or veins of other colors that give marble much of its beauty. These colors range from reds and yellows to greens, black, and browns. No two pieces are ever the same.

If you want to re-create the look of a specific marble, you may need to make several sample pieces until you work out a suitable method. Use either a piece of marble or pictures, which are widely available on Web sites of companies that sell stone.

This project incorporates a variety of techniques so you can see how to create swirls of color, veins, and spots. Many kinds of marble have just one or two of these features, so you can skip some of the steps if you wish to create a look different from the one shown here.

materials and tools

- Base paint (eggshell sheen)
- Glaze
- Paint or universal colorants to tint glaze
- Brush or roller to apply base paint and glaze

- Softening brush or other thick brush with soft bristles
- Spray bottle filled with denatured alcohol
- Round brush or chip brush for spattering

- Veining brush or other thin brush with long bristles
- Disposable gloves
- Cotton T-shirt rags

1. Patch any holes and prime the surface, if necessary. Over that, paint two coats of the base color in an eggshell sheen.

▶ **2.** When the final base coat is dry, prepare a medium glaze (see page 29) in as many colors as needed. Brush individual colors of glaze across the surface in parallel bands, or perhaps diagonally to add interest. Don't worry about making the glaze look even.

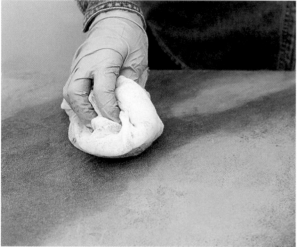

◀**3.** With a cotton rag gathered into a pad or cheesecloth in a pouf (see page 61), dab the glaze to create a mottled look. Dab the rag in and out, rather than rub, so the colors don't blend too much.

▶ **4.** Lightly go over the surface with a softening brush. Alternate between brushing in the direction of the color bands and across them.

▶ **5.** Spritz the surface with denatured alcohol and wait a minute or so until you see the glaze begin to coalesce in some spots and move out of others.

6. Go over the surface with the softening brush again. The alcohol breaks up the glaze and gives the surface a look very similar to some types of marble.

7. To create veins, dip a liner brush—one that's skinny and has long bristles—into a dark glaze and pull the brush toward you as you hold it with your thumb and index finger. Rotate the brush as you pull so the bristles don't flare out.

8. Spread newspaper a few sheets thick. Load a round brush or a chip brush with dark glaze. About 18 inches above the newspaper, flick the bristles with a gloved finger or a small stick. Pull toward you to release a spray of glaze droplets. Practice until you get spots the size you like.

9. Reload the brush and flick the glaze once over the newspaper to release any big drips. Then spatter the surface of your project. Each time you reload the brush, release the first spray over the newspaper.

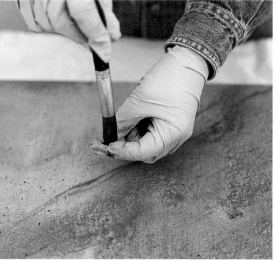

10. Again, go over the area with the softening brush.

METALLIC
effects

Metallic paints aren't just shiny like glossy paint. They also have a pearlescent quality so that the sparkle shifts as you walk past. The glint comes from minute flecks of mica, or fool's gold, that have been coated with a layer of another transparent material.

The metallic look results from the way light changes direction as it passes through the two materials and reflects off them. These mica-based finishes come in gold, silver, and brown shades that resemble various kinds of metal, as well as in colors like purple and green. The vivid colors won't create realistic faux finishes—they're all about fun and fantasy.

In addition, you can buy metallic paints that contain actual metal particles so that they tarnish and rust just as solid metal does. You can let this happen over time or accelerate the process by coating the paint with various patina formulas.

And finally, there is metal leaf. These whisper-thin sheets don't qualify as paint, but they're included in this book because they are another way to transform surfaces and because you may wonder how their effect differs from what you get with metallic paint.

▼ Metallic paint in two Modern Masters colors, Plumb and Pale Gold, livens up this living room. Besides decorating the striped wainscot and the wall above, the mica-rich paint dresses up the fireplace surround and the trim.

▶ Stenciling a design with metallic paint creates a look similar to wallpaper. For an effect like this, choose a large stencil with numerous repeats (see the raised-stencil project on pages 109–111). The colors used in this room are Platinum and Shimmer Sky from Modern Masters. Both get their sparkle from mica.

▼ You can use metallic paints for many of the techniques shown in this book. A dragging technique similar to the one shown on pages 90–91 was used on this wall, for example.

metallic trim

With metallic paint, you often get more impact by using small amounts than you do by covering large areas. Because you notice the paint's contrast with nonmetallic surfaces, not just the inherent shine, metallic paint is particularly effective on trim in rooms where other finishes cover most surfaces. If you use metallic paint on multiple surfaces, such as a wall and its trim, the effect is more muted.

▲ For an understated, somewhat antique look, you can use metallic paint as an accent color. Think of it as painting in shadow lines—except that instead of being on the bottom surface, as a shadow would be, metallic paint belongs on the top, where the highlights are.

◄ With stencils and trim painted in gold metallic paint, this home office looks far from the corporate world.

144

◀ Silver metallic paint pairs well with modern furnishings made at least partly with similarly colored metal, such as aluminum or stainless steel.

▲ Without gold paint, the simple molding in this entryway might look rather ordinary. In gold, however, it gives the room an air of opulence.

◀ A little gilding goes a long way in this elaborate composition of crown molding, stencils, and painted bands.

brushed metal

This project uses metallic paint to simulate the look of
metal that has been polished with a fine wire brush.
The effect looks great in modern spaces.

Because metallic paints get most
of their impact from the way they
reflect light, slight differences in
surface texture are very noticeable.
That fact, plus the relatively thick
consistency of these paints, means
that it's nearly impossible to create a
surface free of brushstrokes or roller
marks, unless you spray the paint.
However, this shouldn't discourage
you from applying metallic paint
with a brush or roller. Just work a
surface texture into your design.

You must start with a smooth
surface to create this effect. If the
wall is textured, see pages 178–179
for a method to smooth it out.

materials and tools

- ◆ Metallic paint
- ◆ Roller with cover
- ◆ Roller tray
- ◆ 4-inch chip brush
- ◆ Cotton T-shirt rags

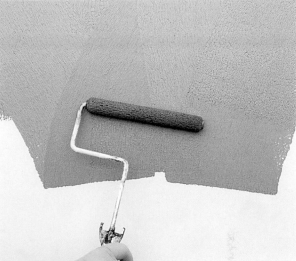

1. Apply primer if the surface hasn't been painted previously or if it has been patched or coated with drywall mud since the last paint was applied.

▶ **2.** When the primer is dry, use a roller to coat an area about 3 by 5 feet with metallic paint.

◀**3.** Immediately go over the area with a dry chip brush. The polishing machines used on real metal rotate, so move your brush in arcs to make the pattern left by the bristles look realistic.

4. Wipe the brush on a clean cotton rag so the bristles don't become clogged with paint. Then repeat steps 2 and 3 on an adjoining area. Brush across the overlaps so the sections blend.

◀**5.** The final result.

hammered metal

Metallic paint applied with a roller will result in tiny humps and divots that look similar to the finish of hammered metal. This project takes advantage of that texture with a counter-top that resembles sheets of metal riveted together.

To emphasize the idea of separate sheets, use several shades of copper and bronze paint.

Like any painted countertop, this one is best where it won't get much abuse. In a kitchen, consider it a short-term solution and add a protective coat or two of acrylic polyurethane. If there is a chance that the counter-top will get wet, use exterior-grade plywood with a smooth overlay as a base. This material, often referred to as MDO (for medium-density overlay) is often sold for making outdoor signs. Press wood filler into any gaps along edges and sand them smooth before you apply the primer. If the countertop is away from water sources, you can use medium-density fiberboard (MDF) or even a hollow-core door that hasn't been drilled for a knob. You can also use this technique to embellish furniture, shelves, or backsplashes.

materials and tools

- Countertop material
- Wood filler, if necessary
- Primer
- Pencil with intact eraser
- Straightedge
- Painter's tape
- Metallic paint
- Roller with covers (one cover per color)
- Paint trays (one per color)
- Black glaze or paint

1. Plug any holes in the countertop with wood filler. When the filler is dry, sand all exposed surfaces. Prime the top, bottom (if accessible), and edges.

▼ **2.** With a pencil and a straightedge, draw a design that resembles a countertop pieced together from metal sheets. Decide which color to use in each section.

▶ **3.** Apply painter's tape around the outside perimeter of as many sections as possible. Because of the space taken up by the tape, you will need to skip over all sections that abut the parts you tape.

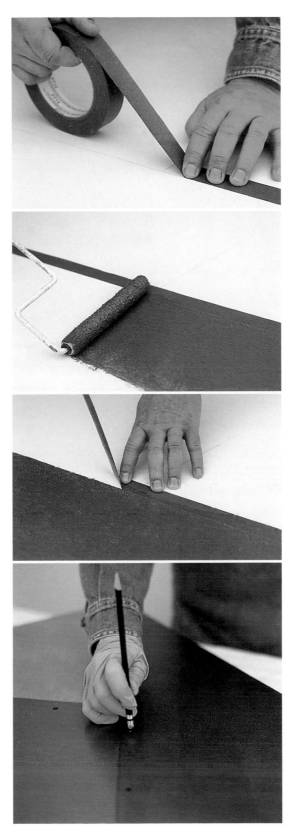

▶ **4.** Roll metallic paint inside the taped areas. In each section, move the roller in parallel lines. You can vary the direction from section to section, however.

▶ **5.** While the paint is still wet, gently remove the tape. Pressing with your finger ahead of the area where you are lifting the tape helps keep underlying paint or primer intact.

6. When paint in the first sections is dry, repeat steps 3 through 5 on areas you skipped.

7. Apply a second coat of paint using the same process. If paint seeps under the tape despite your best efforts to press the edge down securely, coat the tape with the color of the paint that's underneath, as shown on page 71, and wait for that to dry before you paint each area.

▶ **8.** When the paint is dry, add rivets. Use dark-colored glaze or black paint, and apply it with the eraser on the end of a new pencil. Space the dots evenly along the seams between colors.

metallic pot

Metallic paint looks so realistic that you can use it to transform inexpensive objects, such as plastic garden pots, into expensive-looking decorative pieces. If the surface is slick, scuff it up first with sandpaper and use a primer designed to stick to glossy surfaces. Make sure it's a type recommended by the manufacturer of the metallic paint.

You may need a special acid-resistant primer if you will apply a reactive metal paint. This kind of paint, which contains actual metal particles, looks realistic because it tarnishes over time, just as solid metal does. You can rush the patina by applying special acidic solutions made by manufacturers of metal paints. Some patina products result in a green or blue verdigris, while others create black or rust-red areas. Apply the patina material with a brush if you want the entire surface to appear weathered. If you prefer a mottled look, use small pieces of natural sea sponge as an application tool. Wear rubber gloves while you are working with the patina solution.

materials and tools

- Plastic pot
- 100-grit sandpaper
- Primer
- Brush
- Metallic paint (type that accepts a patina solution)
- Patina solution, if desired
- Brush or small pieces of natural sponge
- Disposable gloves

▲ 1. Scuff up the surface by sanding it. Wipe off the dust.

▶ 2. Apply primer to the surface.

▶ 3. When the primer is dry, brush on the metallic paint.

4. When the first coat is dry, add a second coat if you see bare spots.

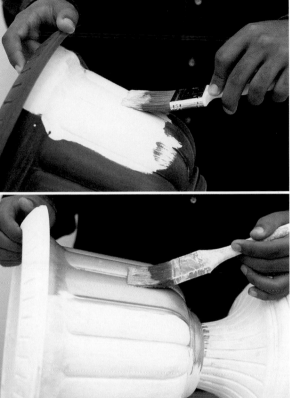

◀ 5. When the second coat is dry, apply a patina solution or a combination of solutions. Where you want the surface to turn color uniformly, fully cover the area with solution.

◀ 6. Where you want more of a mottled look, dab the surface with a piece of sponge that's saturated with the solution. Be sure to wear disposable gloves.

other transformations with metallic paint

Items made of wood, plastic, clay, and glass can be transformed with metallic paint. You can even use it on metal items to convert a shiny brass lamp into one that looks like it's made of iron, for example.

Besides the ideas shown here, you might also consider giving the faux metal treatment to shelf supports and shelving, drapery rods and their finials, stereo speakers, chairs and stools, wooden cabinet knobs, and a wide array of flea market finds. Follow the step-by-step instructions on pages 150–151, except for a few special circumstances.

▲ Two coats of copper paint turned a fencepost topper into an elegant finial. Rubbing the final coat, once it was dry, with a scrub pad removed brush marks and left the surface with a more uniform sheen.

◄ To transform a clay pot, you can brush iron paint directly onto the clay. Avoid covering the surface completely if you want some clay to remain visible. When the paint is dry, dab a rust patina formula onto some but not all areas of the paint. If you use the pot for plants, moisture in the soil will cause all of the paint to rust.

◄ This plant stand began as a disk of plywood, a cardboard form for a concrete foundation pier, and a plastic bowl. To hold the round base to the tube, a wooden plug was screwed to the base and then to the tube. The bowl on top just rests in place. To keep the stand from tipping if a heavy plant is placed in the top, set bags of sand or gravel in the tube.

▶ Brushing blue metallic paint over the inside of a glass vase creates the look of an expensive ceramic piece. The paint layer is relatively fragile but strong enough for displaying dried flowers.

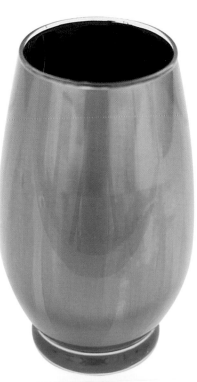

▶ This inexpensive plastic lamp from a thrift store was sanded and primed. When the primer was dry, gold metallic paint was dabbed on lightly so that some of the white primer shows through, creating a mottled effect with the gold.

▲ By cutting a wooden bowl in half and mounting it to a wall, you can create a handy place for stashing keys or other items. This half-bowl was painted black, then brushed lightly with iron paint. Rust patina was applied to that. A coat or two of acrylic polyurethane would protect the finish from being scraped off by keys.

▲ Besides painting molding to look like shiny metal, you can also use reactive metal paint and apply a patina solution to some areas.

gold leaf

A wall covered with whisper-thin sheets of genuine gold, silver, or copper is truly elegant. Composition leaf, made of less expensive metals, is an affordable substitute for the real thing, costing $1 to $2 per square foot. This project combines composition gold leaf with red paint for a royal wall finish.

Composition gold leaf is made from brass, a combination of copper and zinc. Another good option is composition silver, which is actually aluminum. Commonly sold in sheets 5½ inches square, the composition materials have only one drawback: they will eventually tarnish if you leave them exposed to the air. Coating the finished surface with a sealer, such as shellac or acrylic, solves that problem and helps keep the metal from being scraped off.

Red base paint was used here to mimic a long tradition among makers of gilded metal frames. Before they applied the gilding, they often brushed the frame with red bole, a mixture of hide glue and a red earth pigment. Moistening the animal glue created a surface sticky enough to grab onto the gold sheets, and the bits of red that showed where the metal flaked off made the gold look warmer. This project uses the modern alternatives of composition metal leaf and standard red paint.

materials and tools

- Red base paint
- Composition gold leaf
- Adhesive for composition leaf
- Brush or roller to apply adhesive
- 2- or 3-inch foam applicator
- Clear finish, such as shellac or acrylic

1. Brush or roll the red base paint onto the wall. One coat should be enough.

▶ **2.** When the base paint is dry, apply the adhesive, which is often called size, a small section at a time. Use a brush if you want brushstrokes to leave a texture in the gold leaf. If you want a more uniform texture to show, apply the adhesive with a roller.

3. Check the label on the adhesive to see how long you need to wait to apply the leaf. The adhesive must become tacky.

▼ **4.** When the adhesive is ready, carefully pick up a sheet of the composition leaf and its paper overlay. Position the sheet on the wall with the paper side out.

5. Press on the sheet just enough to secure it to the adhesive. Then peel off the tissue cover.

▶ **6.** Using the disposable foam applicator, very gently smooth the leaf and fully press it into the adhesive.

▶ **7.** Where sheets overlap, small pieces of gold leaf will break off and flutter to the floor. Retrieve them and use them to patch bare spots. Just press the patches into the adhesive and lightly brush back and forth with the foam tool.

◀ **8.** Wait for the adhesive to dry completely. Then lightly brush over all the edges of the sheets to remove remaining loose flakes of the leaf. Apply the clear finish with a brush or a roller. If you use shellac, use a roller.

▶ **9.** Stop at this point if you wish. This is the result.

▲ **10.** Or go on to give the surface a slightly antique look. Do this by sanding scattered areas very lightly—just enough to wear off the gold but not the red paint underneath.

▶ **11.** The final result with the antiquing.

smooth edges

WHEN YOU PAINT A SURFACE, the brush or roller marks are always an issue. With metal leaf, edges of the sheets are the telltale marks. To produce the neatest look, align sheets in rows and plan ahead so you don't wind up with partial sheets along just one side of the room. Figure out how many full sheets you need and how much space is left over. Cut partial sheets to fit, then cut them in half. Use them on both sides of the room.

CHOOSING COLORS
for metallic effects

Because they reflect light differently depending on your viewing angle, metallic paints create dramatic effects. Combining them with standard paint in deep tones works well. Or, by using metallic and nonmetallic paint in the same color, you can create designs with metallic paint that are nearly invisible from some angles but bright from others.

BASE PAINT   METALLIC

BASE PAINT   METALLIC

BASE PAINT   METALLIC

BASE PAINT

METALLIC

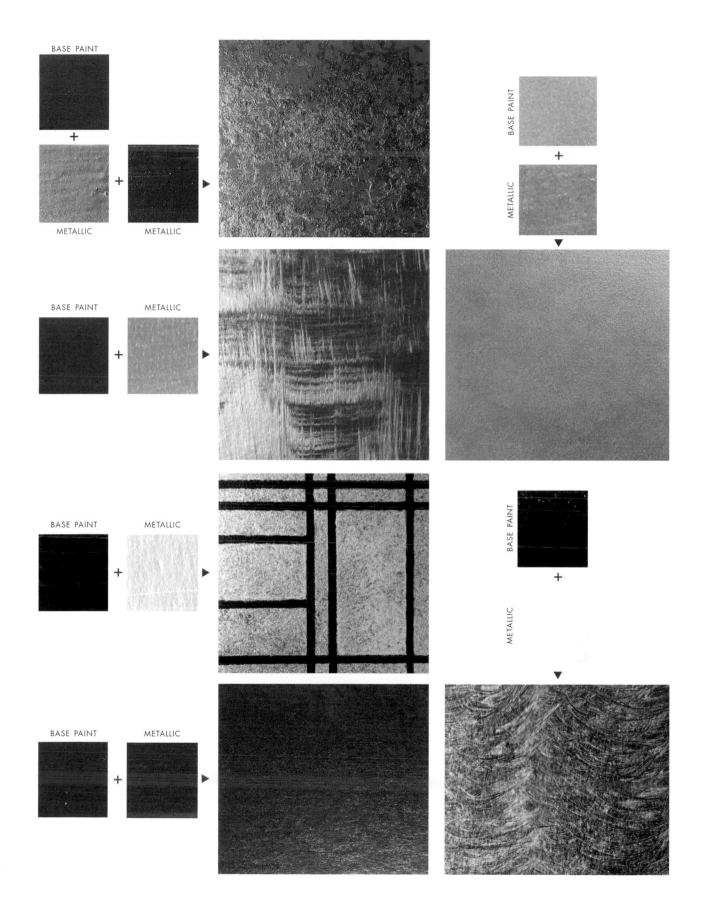

BASE PAINT

+

METALLIC   +   METALLIC

BASE PAINT

+

METALLIC

BASE PAINT   METALLIC

BASE PAINT   METALLIC

BASE PAINT

+

METALLIC

BASE PAINT   METALLIC

ANTIQUE
effects

A few antiquing measures can help relax an overly formal room or an area where surfaces are too pristine for your tastes. On a wall, you might scuff up the paint with sandpaper, as shown in the gold leaf project on pages 154–157, or rub on an umber glaze, like the one applied to the stenciled venetian plaster on pages 118–120. Or you can opt for a crackle finish, which re-creates the alligator-skin look of old, cracked paint.

◄ Weathered barn boards were nailed to this wall, and their distressed look was enhanced with paint.

▲ Truly old, not just trying to look it, a plastered and stenciled wall displays random, varied signs of wear. To be realistic, faux aging needs similar details.

▼ Sandpaper and a dark glaze create instant patina on these kitchen cabinets.

▲ Distressed with sandpaper, a painted and stenciled chest like this one works well in a room with a shabby chic theme.

◄ A crackle finish on trim adds contrast to this room, which also features painted squares on the floor and mottled paint on the walls.

china crackle

Specialty products produced by faux and decorative paint companies are the key to coaxing paint into cracking the way old oil-based paint does. Some products are designed to be brushed over paint, while others go between coats. The difference isn't just in the application method. It also affects the final look.

This project, which involved painting a tiny table to use for children's tea parties, features the type of crackle medium that's painted over an existing finish. Manufacturers use different terms for their products, but this type produces a finer crackle than the other type. Read the label to determine which product you want.

For this effect, you top base paint with a clear coat, then make it crackle. Rubbing glaze into the cracks makes them more noticeable. Because you need proprietary products to create this finish, use the instructions here as a general guide. Follow the label instructions for application and drying time.

materials and tools

- Primer, if necessary
- Base paint, if necessary
- Crackle base coat
- Crackle top coat
- Crackle enhancer or standard glaze tinted in a contrasting color
- Chip brush
- Roller with cover (optional)
- Disposable gloves
- Cotton T-shirt rags

1. If you like the existing color of the object, proceed to the next step. Otherwise, apply primer and two coats of paint. Let each coat dry as the label recommends.

2. Brush or roll on the crackle base coat. Let the material dry for 20 to 40 minutes, until it feels slightly sticky but leaves no residue on your hand. You can use a hair dryer set to medium to speed up the process. Hold the dryer 10 to 12 inches from the surface.

▶ **3.** Carefully brush on the crackle top coat. Brush in one direction and go over each area only once or the crackle effect won't be uniform.

4. Allow the second coat to dry thoroughly, which may take 1 to 2 hours. You can use the hair dryer for this step as well.

◀ **5.** Apply crackle enhancer. If you have glaze left over from another project, you can use it instead. Tint the glaze in a color that contrasts with the base coat.

tip CRACKLE EFFECTS LOOK best on woodwork, such as trim, furniture, and cabinets, because oil-based paint was traditionally used on these surfaces. Crackle looks odd on a wall and is difficult to apply there evenly. Also, the cracks cause problems if the room is repainted, as they will show through unless the wall is first sanded smooth or coated with drywall mud.

▲ **6.** With a clean cotton cloth, wipe off most of the glaze, leaving what has settled into the crevices.

aged crackle

This type of crackle finish mimics the look of old oil paint that has cracked and fallen away in sections. The cracks are deeper, and the pieces of intact paint are larger and more irregular than they are with china crackle.

For this effect, first apply a base layer, which is the color that will eventually show in the cracks. Then brush on the crackle medium (which manufacturers also call aging or weathering medium) and wait for it to partially dry. Finally, a second color of paint goes on. Cheap, flat paint works best. Cracks will appear before your eyes as the paint from the second coat moves around, opening up to show the base coat.

Choose an object with fairly simple lines. Because the second coat slides around, apply the final two layers only to horizontal surfaces to get the most even results. Wait for those to dry, then rotate the object.

materials and tools

- Primer, if necessary
- Base paint
- Aged crackle medium
- Top paint (flat sheen)
- Rollers, if desired (³⁄₈-inch nap for base paint, ¹⁄₄-inch nap for crackle glaze)
- Roller tray (if you are using rollers)
- Brush
- Clear finish, such as acrylic
- Polyurethane

1. If the piece is painted a color that would work well in the cracks, proceed to step 2. Otherwise, apply primer, if necessary, and a coat of paint in the color you want the cracks to be. Let the paint dry for at least 4 hours.

▲ **2.** With a brush or the ¼-inch-nap roller, apply the crackle medium to all horizontal surfaces. Apply the material as uniformly as you can, but move in only one direction and go over each area only once. If you skip a small area, either touch it up with a narrow brush or leave it. Don't go over coated areas a second time.

▲ **3.** When the crackle medium has dried as long as the label recommends, perhaps 1 to 4 hours, carefully apply the top paint with a brush or the ⅜-inch-nap roller. The brush width affects the width of the cracks. Again, work in one direction and go over each area only one time. Be careful not to overlap paint. If you miss an area, leave it as it is. You can touch it up with crackle and top paint after the initial finish is dry.

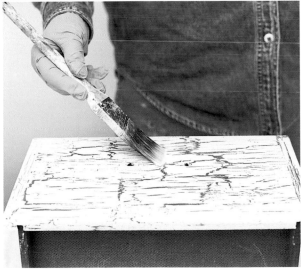

4. Allow the object to sit undisturbed until the finish is dry, then rotate the object and repeat steps 2 and 3 for surfaces that are now horizontal. Repeat until you have created a crackle finish on the entire object.

▲ **5.** With a brush or the ⅜-inch-nap roller, apply a clear finish to seal the edges of the crackled paint.

lime paint AND lime wash

Most of the water-based paint used today leaves a thin plastic finish on walls or other surfaces. But there are other types of water-based paint, including milk paint, based on the casein protein in milk; distemper, based on hide glue; and lime paint, based on slaked lime.

Lime paint in particular offers wonderful advantages in certain interior decorating projects. The paint dries to a very flat finish, with the color varying from dark to light across the surface. It's the authentic subtle mottled look.

Lime wash is a faux product that simulates the brushstrokes that can be created with lime paint. Use it in combination with standard wall paint.

▲ Lime paint naturally develops a somewhat mottled look, but you can heighten the contrast by brushing or sponging on a slightly different color.

◀ Because lime paint is a traditional material, it looks particularly good when tinted with pigments that are dug from the earth and crushed. The original red pigment was soil rich in iron, which naturally rusts. The yellow most common in house paint came from ochre deposits, which contain a hydrated form of iron oxide.

▼ You can combine other decorative paint techniques, such as stenciling, with lime wash and lime paint. This design was made with lime paint.

◀ When you use lime paint, you usually tint it yourself with powdered pigments. This allows you to adjust the intensity as you wish. Colors can be deeply saturated, as the blue on this wall is, or extremely pale. Untinted lime paint is white and does not yellow with age.

lime paint

Traditionally, lime paint has been used mostly over porous masonry surfaces, including cement plaster and adobe. Modern formulations, many of which contain small amounts of acrylic, can go over drywall. Because lime paint is applied with a wide brush and contains minerals that give it body, you can use it to create both smooth surfaces and textured ones where brushstrokes show.

This project has a smooth finish. The dead-flat paint and the varying color intensity create a look with the cushy depth of velvet. It makes you want to reach out and touch the wall to feel the texture. But all your fingers will detect is a smooth surface.

Lime paint remains somewhat porous, which makes it very popular in buildings where the walls must breathe, such as those built of straw bales. However, if you use this paint where there will be fingerprints or food spatters, you will discover the downside of porous coatings: they stain. Apply a clear finish, such as acrylic, to protect the paint.

Lime paint formulations vary by manufacturer. Read the label for specific instructions about surface preparation. Some formulas develop rich color faster if they are applied over a skim coat of drywall mud rather than primer.

materials and tools

- Primer, if needed
- Drywall mud, if needed
- Lime paint
- Powdered pigments
- Stir stick or 1-inch round brush
- Lime brush or other big brush with natural bristles
- Painter's tape
- Disposable gloves
- Disposable respirator that protects against fine particles

1. Mask trim with painter's tape. If the wall has a textured finish and you want smooth lime paint, or if you have smooth walls and want quick color saturation, skim-coat the surface with drywall mud. When the coating is dry, put on a respirator and sand it smooth. Vacuum off the dust.

◄**2.** Again, put on a disposable respirator and leave it on while you are working with dry pigment. To tint the paint, measure equal amounts of water and pigment. A medium tone requires ¼ cup of pigment per quart of lime paint. Pour the water into a container big enough to hold all the paint you will need for your project.

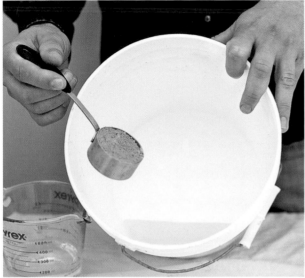

▶ **3.** Add the pigment to the water and stir. You can use a stir stick, but a brush works better because the bristles help break up clumps of pigment.

▶ **4.** When no visible lumps remain, the pigment mixture will still look grainy, but it is ready to be combined with the paint.

◄**5.** Stir lime paint into the pigment mixture until everything is thoroughly combined.

◄**6.** Apply the paint using the lime brush for large areas and the round, pointed brush for corners and tight spots. Working across the wall, apply the paint with a series of overlapping X's. Work the paint into the wall one area at a time. Cupping your hand over the brush helps you get the right pressure. If you want a smooth surface without visible brush marks, go over the painted area with the brush nearly flat to the wall and make a lighter series of crosshatches. Brushing with only the tips of the bristles also makes brushstrokes less visible.

▶**7.** When the first coat is dry, apply a second coat. Repeat step 6 unless you want to see brushstrokes in the finish. In that case, skip the final feathering with the brush.

▼**8.** If you want a slightly shiny surface that shows greater color variation, burnish the paint once it is thoroughly dry. Use a flat trowel, like one you'd use for venetian plaster. Move it in circles over the surface. Press with both hands on the trowel.

▼**9.** If the surface is likely to collect spatters or fingerprints, protect the paint with a clear sealer, such as acrylic. Use the lime brush and the same technique that you used for the lime paint so that you don't alter the texture of the surface.

lime wash

Lime wash is a texture material that mimics the look of lime paint. It's designed to be used with standard water-based paint and is also compatible with water-based glazes.

Apply it over a surface that has already been painted the basic color that you want. The lime wash will dry white and create a chalky-looking haze as well as a light texture on the wall. It can be left as is. If you want to emphasize the texture or add more color variation, you can coat it with a glaze. Or apply glaze and rub most of it off, leaving only small amounts caught in the raised designs from the lime wash.

materials and tools

- Primer, if needed
- Roller with cover and tray for base paint
- Base paint (any sheen)
- Lime wash
- Wide, thick brush
- Cotton T-shirt rags
- Glaze
- Paint or tint to color the glaze

1. Apply primer, if needed. When that is dry, apply base paint with a roller.

▶ **2.** When the base paint is dry, brush the lime wash onto the wall. First dab it on in scattered sections. Then blend the colors by rapidly brushing over the entire area with a series of overlapping X's.

▶ **3.** If you want to add color and emphasize the texture, prepare a transparent to medium glaze (see page 29). Brush it on with a wide, thick brush. Repeat the X's you made when you applied the lime wash, but there's no need to match them exactly.

▶ **4.** Go over the surface with a soft cotton rag. This will cause glaze to catch in crevices of the lime wash and make the texture more obvious.

5. The resulting finish resembles a mottled wall, but because it's really textured, the surface reflects light differently than one that's merely decorated with paint.

PREPARING
to paint

YOU'RE LUCKY IF YOU CAN begin painting right away, the dream
scenario detailed in chapter 1. Often, though, you'll have to do
considerable prep work first. This chapter helps you understand when
that's needed and how to do it. You'll find tips about patching holes
in drywall and plaster walls, selecting the right primer, and painting
surfaces other than walls, such as ceilings, doors, and windows. Because
many of the decorative paint techniques covered in chapter 2 must be
done on smooth surfaces, you will also find information about how to
smooth out textured walls.

▶ It's important to prime surfaces that have been sanded, that
are going from oil to latex paint, or that are going from dark
to light colors. See pages 180–181 for more information.

PATCHING
holes

Drywall, which consists of a gypsum core sandwiched between two sheets of paper, is soft and vulnerable to damage. Fortunately, drywall is also relatively easy to repair. You can fill nail holes with lightweight spackling compound, which has the consistency of whipped cream. Use spackling paste to fill dents. To repair larger holes, use drywall joint compound over an appropriate patching material.

PATCHING DENTS AND DINGS

If the drywall is dented but other-wise intact, the repair is simple.

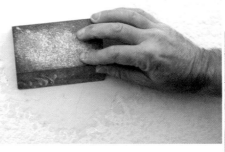

▲ 1. Stir the spackling paste to a creamy consistency. With a 3-inch drywall knife, press the material into the hole and smooth the surface. Spackling paste must be applied in layers no more than ¼ inch deep, so if the ding is deep, you will need to apply a second layer after the first one dries.

▲ 2. When the final coat is dry, sand the spot with 220-grit sandpaper or a sanding block.

▶ 3. If the wall has a textured finish, apply a spray-on texture material or the smooth patch will be noticeable even after you repaint. Test the spray on cardboard first to determine how far from the surface you must hold the can for the best match. To keep the distance uniform, move your whole body with the can while spraying straight at the wall; don't pivot from side to side, which would make the stream come from different distances. Overlap your passes by about one-third. When you're finished, clean the nozzle by turning the can upside down and spraying at the cardboard test piece until texture material stops coming out.

tip WHILE YOU'RE PATCHING HOLES, also check whether screws or nails have popped loose from the drywall. Tighten screws with a screwdriver or drive nails with a hammer so the heads are just below the surface of the drywall. Then cover the indentations with spackle. If you accidentally tear the drywall paper as you set the fasteners, cover the patch with fiberglass mesh and proceed as if you were patching a small hole.

PATCHING SMALL HOLES When the damage extends all the way through the drywall, you can't just swipe spackle over the hole, as there's no backing to hold the patch in place. Use a drywall patching kit, which contains a small piece of fiberglass mesh, often attached to a stiff material that fortifies the patch.

▶ **1.** Use a utility knife to cut away torn edges of the drywall paper and any loose bits of the gypsum.

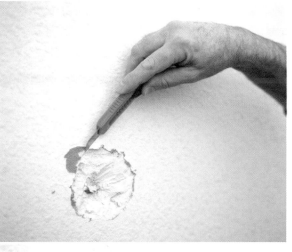

▶ **2.** Place the patch material over the hole. Smooth out the mesh and press it down. Avoid creating wrinkles. The patch should extend an inch beyond all edges of the hole.

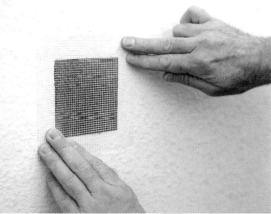

◀ **3.** Stir drywall mud to a creamy consistency. With a 3-inch drywall knife, butter it over the patch.

4. When the first layer is dry, knock off any ridges with the drywall knife, or sand the patch lightly with 150-grit sandpaper or a sanding block.

▶ **5.** Add a second coat of drywall mud over a slightly larger area, using a wider taping knife if you have one. If you don't own this tool, you can get by without it, but the next step may take longer because you'll have more ridges in the mud.

6. When the patch is dry, sand the area.

7. Apply texture material following the tips in step 3 on page 174.

PATCHING LARGER HOLES

Patching large holes isn't as hard as you might think. The hardest part may be finding a scrap of drywall so that you don't need to buy a full 4-by-8-foot sheet. Some building-materials companies sell small pieces or may be willing to give you part of a damaged sheet. You can also ask friends who are working on their houses or inquire whether a local dry-wall company has any scraps.

▶ **2.** Place the patch over the hole and score around it with a utility knife or box cutter.

▼ **3.** Set aside the patch and gradually deepen its outline until you can remove all of the drywall within that area.

◀ **1.** Using the hole as your guide, cut a rectangular patch that completely covers the hole. Slice through the paper on the front face with a sharp utility knife or box cutter. Snap the sides apart, as if you were making a sample board with a corner (see page 41). Then cut through the back paper.

▶ **4.** Cut a plywood scrap big enough to span the hole but with enough of a clearance that you can hold the piece in place as you screw the surrounding dry-wall to it. If the patch is near a stud, you might need to orient the plywood vertically. Add several screws so the plywood is attached firmly. Drive screw heads slightly below the drywall surface, but not so deep that the paper tears.

▶ **5.** Screw the drywall patch onto the plywood.

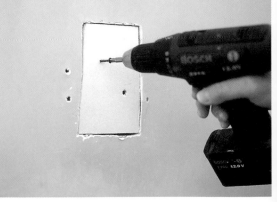

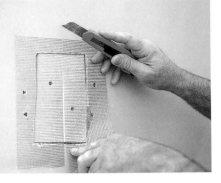

▲ **6.** Cover the patch and a 1-inch perimeter around it with fiberglass mesh, which is sold for covering seams between sheets. If the mesh has an adhesive backing, just press it onto the wall. If not, use a 3-inch drywall knife to cover the area with a thin layer of drywall mud and then immediately press the mesh into that. Instead of the mesh, you can use plastic window screening.

▲ **7.** With a 3-inch drywall knife, cover the area with drywall mud.

8. When the mud is dry, usually in 24 hours, knock off ridges with the drywall knife or lightly sand with 150-grit sandpaper or a sanding block. Coat a slightly larger area with more drywall mud and feather out the edges. If the size of the patch warrants it, use a 6-inch taping knife to smooth the second layer and go on to do a third layer, over an even larger area, with a 12-inch taping knife.

9. Sand the patch smooth and apply drywall texture, if needed (see page 174).

PATCHING PLASTER Walls in many older houses are covered with plaster, not drywall. Behind the plaster there are either thin wooden slats, known as lath, or metal mesh.

Plaster repairs begin differently than drywall repairs, though the final steps of sanding and texturing are the same. Because plaster is hard and therefore not as easily damaged as drywall, you should first question why the damage has occurred and fix the underlying problem before you patch. If the plaster is stained brown, there was probably a water leak. Unless there's been an earthquake, numerous cracks could point to a structural problem, which a home inspector or a builder may help you pinpoint.

With plaster, you must always remove or secure all loose material first. For small patches, removal works best. For larger repairs, you may be able to reattach the plaster to wood lath by using screws with wide washers under the heads. Or replace the plaster with drywall.

To fix a small crack, use the pointed end of a painter's 5-in-1 tool to remove all loose plaster and dig out a crevice that's wider at the back than on the front of the wall. Dampen the plaster around the hole, then fill the crack with lightweight spackling compound. If the crack is more than ¼ inch wide, use patching plaster.

▲ Fill small holes in plaster walls with spackling compound.

To patch a larger hole, cut wire mesh or hardware cloth larger than the hole and thread a tie wire through it. Push the mesh through the hole. Hold on to the wire and wrap it around a stick that spans the hole. This keeps the mesh in place while you dampen the hole and fill it partway with patching plaster. When the material is dry, clip off the wire and add plaster coats until the surface is smooth and level.

If the lath is still intact, you can also use drywall to patch the hole. Excavate a rectangular area of the plaster. Press a sheet of paper over the hole and crease along its edges. Using this as a pattern, cut a patch of drywall 2 inches oversize in all directions. Within the 2-inch border, cut through the back of the drywall and through the gypsum to make a rectangle that matches the hole. Leave the face paper intact as you peel off the border. You can then use the drywall with the paper extension to patch the wall as if you were using a repair kit.

SMOOTHING OUT
a textured wall

In many homes, walls have a noticeable texture. If you want to try one of the special effects shown in this book that requires a smooth surface, you might be able to sand the wall flat. But if there are many layers of paint, this can be difficult and messy. The following method, called skim coating, usually works better.

1. Cover the floor with a drop cloth and mask off trim or other areas you want to protect.

▶ **2.** Mix drywall mud to a creamy consistency. The amount of mud you will need depends on how much texture is on the wall. If you are mixing a large quantity, save a lot of effort by using a paddle mixer attached to a drill.

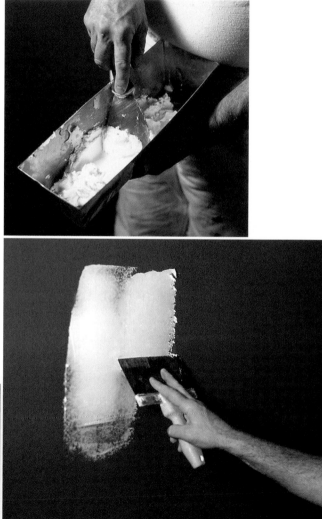

▶ **3.** With a 6-inch taping knife, apply just enough of the mud to the wall to completely cover the texture. Make vertical passes.

◀**4.** After you have applied mud to a section, smooth it with a wider taping knife. Or use a venetian plaster trowel. Don't worry about leaving small ridges.

5. While the mud dries, tape up plastic drop cloths to isolate the area where you are working so fine dust particles don't travel through your house. Seal all edges with tape. So you can get in and out, overlap sheets at one doorway or tape on a zipper that paint stores sell for this purpose.

6. When the mud is dry, perhaps in 24 hours, scrape across the wall with a wide taping knife to knock off ridges. If you see small holes in the surface, fill them in with another thin layer of joint compound.

7. Sand the surface smooth using one of the methods described at right.

8. Vacuum the walls before you paint.

sanding drywall mud

WHEN YOU HAVE a lot of drywall mud to sand, it makes sense to do it as quickly as possible in a way that generates minimal dust. If you use a method below that does generate dust, wear goggles and a disposable respirator (the double-elastic type, not a flimsy dust mask). If you're working overhead, a hat helps too.

SANDPAPER Fold sandpaper in quarters or use a sanding block. Start with 120-grit and finish with 150-grit. This is the messiest approach, but it uses the least equipment and results in a fine finish.

SCREENING Pros often use an abrasive screen fitted on the end of a pole. This speeds the work and results in a finish similar to what you get with sandpaper. You avoid a lot of work from a ladder but put more strain on your arms and back.

VACUUM SANDING You can buy or rent sanders that attach to vacuums. This adds to the expense and noise, but the work goes swiftly and there's very little dust.

WET SANDING With a small-cell polyurethane sponge made for this purpose, you can sand drywall mud by hand without generating dust. This is a simple, inexpensive, and quiet solution, though it leaves the surface slightly rougher than 150-grit sandpaper does.

THE IMPORTANCE
of primer

Priming walls before you put on the final color may seem like a waste of time and money, but in many cases, it's just the opposite: Primer cuts down on how many top coats you need to get an even finish. Many of the stories you may have heard about needing four or more coats of paint to cover a surface can be traced to a lack of primer.

tip PAINT STORES CAN TINT most primers but the resulting shades are often pastels. Nevertheless, use tinted primer when possible. A little color helps you achieve an even shade in the finish paint.

Primer and finish paint are formulated differently because they serve different purposes. Primers stick, block stains, and seal surfaces so they are evenly porous. Top coats add color and durability. They stand up to sunlight and can be scrubbed clean.

Use primer when dealing with:

- New drywall
- Patched drywall or plaster
- Slick surfaces (glossy paint, laminate, glass, plastic)
- Stains from water, smoke, or other causes
- A switch in paint types (from oil- to water-based)
- Dramatic color changes
- Unpainted wood
- Previously painted wood where pitch or knots show

Applying primer involves the same steps as applying finish paint. See pages 43–49 for specifics.

▲ Primer costs less than paint, so it makes a wise first coat when you are painting over a vivid design or are switching from a dark-colored wall to one that's light. This primer was tinted.

CHOOSING THE RIGHT PRIMER

surface	issue	solution
new drywall	The paper face and joint compound over seams absorb paint at different rates.	Use polyvinyl acetate (PVA) primer, a water-based product.
patched drywall or plaster	The joint compound or spackling paste is porous, but the surrounding paint is not, so they absorb paint at different rates.	Use a general-purpose, water-based primer, assuming the existing paint and the new top coat are both water based.
slick surfaces	Finish paint has a hard time grabbing onto a surface where there is no "tooth," so it doesn't adhere.	Use a water-based primer labeled as suitable for slick surfaces. An alcohol-based primer with shellac also works, but it smells stronger and makes cleanup more difficult.
stained surfaces	You paint over stains and all looks good. But when the paint dries, the stains reappear. The reason is that water-soluble stains travel right through standard water-based primers and mar the finish paint. Oily stains are also problematic, as the new paint skids off.	For mild stains, use a water-based primer labeled as a stain blocker. Severe stains require an oil-based, stain-blocking primer, or an alcohol-based primer with shellac. To determine whether you can use a water based primer, test a section by painting the dry primer with top coat. If the stain reappears, switch to an oil or alcohol primer.
different base paint	Oil paint continues to harden as it ages, while water-based paint remains somewhat flexible. Particularly when the oil paint is glossy, this can keep the layers from bonding properly, which may cause the top coat to peel off if it is scratched.	Use a general-purpose water-based primer or one formulated for blocking stains.
unpainted wood	Standard paint doesn't bond sufficiently to bare wood to keep up with the wood's expansion and contraction as humidity shifts, so the paint is likely to peel. Also, some wood, especially cedar and redwood, contains water-soluble ingredients, known as tannins, that stain water-based paint. And woods such as oak and ash have open pores that absorb paint and make it difficult to achieve a smooth top coat.	Use a general-purpose water-based primer in most cases, but go for one labeled as an "enamel undercoat" if you want an especially glassy surface. Before you prime, dampen the wood and wait 30 minutes for the surface fibers to swell. Sand them off, then prime. Otherwise they will swell within the primer and make the surface fuzzy. Or use an alcohol- or oil-based primer, which prevents the problem. On open-pore woods, use a paste filler before you prime.
pitch pockets and knots	Sticky pitch, common in knots but also found in isolated patches within wood, can bleed through paint and mar the surface.	Prime the entire surface with an alcohol-based primer with shellac. Or spot-prime knot holes and pitch pockets with this primer, let that dry, then prime the entire surface with a general-purpose water- or oil-based primer.

PAINTING SURFACES
other than walls

Painting ceilings, doors, and other architectural details involves many of the same steps as painting walls. Review pages 42–49 for step-by-step instructions on basic painting techniques, such as how to apply masking and how to properly load a roller and paintbrush. In this section you will find specific instructions for painting a variety of surfaces.

HOW TO PAINT A CEILING There are two big challenges: minimizing the number of times you need to climb up and down a ladder, and working quickly enough that one area doesn't dry before you paint the adjoining area, which could leave streaks.

Because paint drips downward, it makes sense to work from the top down. The following directions assume you are painting the ceiling in preparation for painting walls. If you are painting only the ceiling, you should mask at least the top edge of the walls in order to protect them from spatters.

1. Prepare for painting. Move as much furniture as possible out of the room and cover the rest with plastic. Cover the floor with drop cloths. Shut off power to the electrical circuit that supplies ceiling fixtures. Depending on their type, you can then either remove them or unscrew each cover plate and wrap it and the fixture in a plastic bag.

▶ **2.** Prepare painting tools so nothing delays you once you begin. You may wish to screw a cup hook (right) onto your brush so you can hook it over a paint can as you climb up and down a ladder to cut in along edges. Slightly dampen the bristles and a roller so they are easier to clean later. Attach an extension handle to the roller, if you have one. Fill a paint tray partway.

◀ **3.** With a brush or a paint pad, cut in at the edges of the ceiling and any architectural detailing there. If you are using ceiling paint or another flat paint, you can do all the edges at once. Otherwise, work in sections so that the edge paint doesn't dry before you get to step 4.

▶ **4.** Roll on paint, working in relatively straight lines across the ceiling. Roll in the direction of the room's shorter dimension, if possible, so the paint is less likely to dry in one section before you get to the next one.

HOW TO PAINT A DOOR With a door, you can remove it and paint it flat or leave it in place. The first approach may be the best in theory because it minimizes drips. But for most people the latter method is faster and safer because there is no heavy lifting or risk of damaging the hinges.

Glossy paint is often found on doors because it stands up better to periodic scrubbing away of fingerprints. To enable new paint to stick to old glossy paint, you could apply a primer designed for slick surfaces, but this adds a layer that will slightly clog some of the door's architectural detailing.

The following approach prevents this and is simpler and faster. The existing paint must be intact and the same type as the new paint.

These steps are for covering panel doors. If you are painting a flat door, work from the top down.

► **2.** Remove the doorknob or leave it in place and mask it with painter's tape. The latter approach is faster and easier, especially with complicated hardware. If the tape pulls away from the metal, apply additional pieces.

◄ **1.** Wearing gloves, wash the door with a TSP-type cleaner. When the surface dries, scuff up the paint by lightly sanding with 180-grit sandpaper or a sanding pad. Do not sand through the finish. Vacuum or wipe off the debris. (Don't sand if the old paint contains lead.)

◄ **3.** Slightly dampen a paintbrush and a "weenie" roller. With the brush, paint the outer left, right, and top edges of the door. Brush lightly along each edge to even out the paint. When you are done with each edge, run a dry brush along the corners to smooth out any drips.

4. Working on one panel at a time, brush paint around the bevel.

5. With the small roller, paint the panel. Using a roller is easier and faster than brushing, and it helps ensure an even coat. If you don't want the slightly pebbly texture that a roller leaves, brush over the paint after you roll it on.

6. After you paint all the panels, brush paint around the handle or knob.

7. Finally, paint the flat areas around the panels with the roller (followed by the brush, if you wish). If there is a vertical piece in the middle of the top of the door, paint it first. Next paint the top horizontal piece, then the outside verticals down as far as the next horizontal. Work your way down the door in this fashion so that you wind up with brushstrokes in the same direction as the wood grain.

8. Inspect for drips and remove any with a flick of the brush. Avoid touching up thin or slightly messy areas. Wait until the paint dries and add a second coat if necessary.

HOW TO PAINT A WINDOW

Many modern windows don't need paint except on the trim, a straightforward job. Painting older windows is more complicated. The following steps cover windows on which only the bottom sash moves. If both sections move, lower the top and raise the bottom so you can paint the hard-to-reach parts before you embark on the rest of the job.

If you suspect the old paint was applied before 1978, test for lead before you begin. If it is present, avoid sanding and remove any loose paint by wiping it away, not vacuuming.

◄ **1.** Scrape off any loose paint. Pay particular attention to sections next to the glass at the lower edge of each pane, where moisture collects.

▼ **2.** If you see mildew, wipe off as much as possible with a damp rag. Remove the remaining stain with a solution of 3 parts water to 1 part bleach. Rinse with clear water.

◄ **3.** Lightly sand the old paint just enough to scuff up its surface, or wash it with a TSP-type cleaner. Don't scratch the glass or etch it with the cleaner.

▲ **4.** Vacuum or wipe off any sanding debris.

▶ **5.** Fill any holes with spackle (lightweight or regular).

▼ **6.** Apply a thin bead of caulk to the bottom of the window frame.

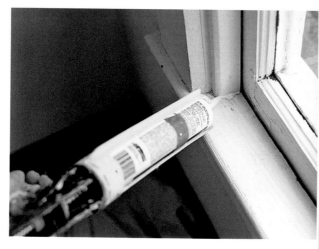

▶ **7.** Remove excess caulk with a drywall knife.

▶ **8.** Apply painter's tape to the glass and to the wall next to the window.

◀**9.** Brush primer over any bare spots or areas you filled with spackle. If you are switching from oil- to water-based paint, prime the entire surface.

◀**10.** When the primer is dry, begin applying the finish paint. Work from the inside out, starting with the beveled area next to the glass.

◀**11.** Avoid depositing globs of paint into the channel where the window moves up and down. Start the brush at that edge and pull the paint away.

12. Remove the tape. If paint seeped under it onto the glass, wait a few days for the paint to harden before you remove it with a new, single-edge razorblade. Dampen the glass before you scrape.

painting vinyl and aluminum windows

THOUGH IT'S NOT NECESSARY to paint vinyl or aluminum windows, you can if you wish to change their look. Scuff up the surface with an abrasive pad, but avoid scratching the glass. Then wash the frame. Use TSP-type cleaner on vinyl, and water with a little vinegar on aluminum. Rinse with clear water. Paint with a water-based primer suitable for slick surfaces, then with a water-based top coat. Because vinyl and aluminum both expand a lot as they get hot, and because dark colors absorb more heat from sunlight than light colors, it's best to stick with relatively light shades.

RESOURCE
guide

MANUFACTURERS OF SPECIALTY PAINTS AND FINISHES

Behr Process Corporation
(800) 854-0133
www.behr.com

Benjamin Moore & Co.
(800) 344-0400
www.benjaminmoore.com

Faux Effects International Inc.
(800) 270-8871
www.fauxeffects.com

The Flood Company
Floetrol® and Penetrol® paint
extenders
(800) 321-3444
www.flood.com

Modern Masters
(800) 942-3166
www.modernmastersinc.com

Ochres & Oxides
(360) 466-1203
www.ochresandoxides.com

Olivetti Mineral Finishes LLC
Lime paint; purchase from
Environmental Home Center
(800) 281-9785
www.environmentalhomecenter.com

Ralph Lauren Paint
(800) 379-POLO
www.rlhome.polo.com

Sherwin-Williams
(800) 474-3794
www.sherwin-williams.com

Valspar
McCloskey Special Effects
(faux line)
(800) 845-9061
www.valspar.com

DECORATIVE PAINTING TOOLS

Bestt Liebco
Symphony™ brand brushes,
rollers, combs, etc.
(800) 523-9095
www.besttliebco.com

The Woolie Inc.
Two-color roller
(763) 541-9534
www.woolie.com

Purdy
(503) 286-8217
www.purdycorp.com

THE FOLLOWING PROFESSIONALS AND BUSINESSES ASSISTED IN THE CREATION OF THIS BOOK:

Patricia Rushon
Refined Finishes
Bainbridge Island, WA
(206) 842-6174
www.refinedfinishes.com

Anna Tofani
Green Door Interior Painting
Bainbridge Island, WA
(206) 780-7935

Interiors Only
Bainbridge Island, WA
(360) 394-1739
www.interiorsonlypainting.com

Mary Jane Rehm Color Consulting
Bainbridge Island, WA
(206) 842-7481

Catherine Mitchell
Interior design
Bainbridge Island, WA
(206) 842-6499

Winslow Paint Company
Bainbridge Island, WA
(206) 842-2227
www.winslowpaint.com

CREDITS

B = bottom; L = left; M = middle;
R = right; T = top

PHOTOGRAPHY CREDITS

Unless otherwise credited, all
photographs are by Chuck Kuhn.

Jean Allsopp: 125B; beateworks.com/
Philip Wegener: 8T; beateworks.
com/Tim Street-Porter: 4–5, 9B;
Courtesy of Benjamin Moore:
32M, 32B; Brian Vanden Brink: 14B,
15MR, 15B, 102R, 104TR, 104BL,
127M, 145BL; Kimberley Burch:
66–67, 84–85, 100–101, 158–159;
Jayson Carpenter: 47, 71, 97; david
duncanlivingston.com: 7R, 9T, 9M,
13TR, 13BR, 14T, 18B, 20B, 22B,
23TR, 24B, 25R, 28–29, 32T, 34B,
51R, 58, 62TR, 68BL, 102L, 113BL,
144R, 145R; Phillip Ennis: 7BL, 8B,
11BL, 15TR, 68TL, 80, 86L, 86R, 88,
90, 105B, 113TL, 113BR, 143B, 157B;
Cheryl Fenton: 31TL; Jamie Hadley:
126L; Philip Harvey: 26; Scott Hirko:
177R; Rob Karosis: 7T, 34T, 56L, 56R,
69L, 69BR, 103TL, 112L, 112R, 146,
160T; Dennis Krukowski: 13L, 27BR,
57R, 75, 87T, 103BL, 104BR, 105TL,
105TR, 126R, 127B, 154, 160B; E.
Andrew McKinney: 87B; courtesy
of Modern Masters: 6R, 33B, 142,
143T; Daniel Nadelbach: 161BR;
Roger Turk/Northlight Photography: 12L, 17T; David Phelps: 10T;
Eric Roth: 12R, 16L, 17B, 21R;
Michael Skott: 10B, 16R, 19T, 161L;
Thomas J. Story: 11TR, 49B, 98, 99B;
Courtesy of Valspar: 33T, 166L; Jessie
Walker: 6L, 11BR, 18T, 21TL, 22T,
24T, 25L, 27TL, 57L, 60, 69TR, 103R,
127T, 144L, 145TL; David Stark
Wilson: 23B; Karen Witynski: 31R,
113TR, 161TR, 166R, 167T, 167B

DESIGN CREDITS

4–5: Franklin Israel, architect; 6L:
David Ogden, Raino-Ogden Associates,
Chicago, Il; 7BL: Michael Murphy;
7T: Cathleen Quandt, architect; 8B:
Interior Consultants, NY; 10T: Jim
Davis, designer/builder; 11BL: Design
Consultants, NJ; 11BR: Kim Elia,
Truffles, Naperville, Il; 12L: Hill
Custom Homes; 12R: Susan Sargent;
13L: wirthsalander.com, designer and
artist; 15TR: Design I, NJ; 16L: Susan
Sargent; 17B: Susan Sargent; 17T: Ann
Gordinier Interior Design; 18T: Gayla
Bailey; 21R: Susan Sargent; 21TL:
Lisbon Interiors, Glenview, Il; 22T:
Kim Elia, Truffles, Naperville, Il; 23B:
David Stark Wilson, dswdesign.com;
24T: paint by Mona Lisa Designs, kit-
chen design by Star Norini-Johnson of
Distinctive Kitchen Designs Inc.; 25L:
Christine Baumbach, Oak Park, Il; 26:
Mona Branagh, Pacific Interiors; 27BR:
Toni Spottswood Interior Design and
Space Planning, NY, Deborah Koster-
Simon, artist; 27TL: Anita Phillipsborn;
31R: Casa Yucatan, Gibbs Smith
Publisher, 2002; 31TL: Annie Cronin,
Verde Design and Janet Costa, A Work
of Art; 34T: David Farmer, architect/
builder; 56L: Dix Shevalier, architect;
56R: Ken Dahlin, architect; 57L:
Anthony Costanza, Oxford, WI; 57R:
Robert Logsdon, artist; 68TL: O'dile
De S., Inc.; 69BR: Scott Henningsen,
architect/builder; 69L: David Farmer,
architect/builder; 69TR: Kathy
McDonald ASID, St. Charles, Il; 75:
Joanna Seitz/Marcia Litwin, Melinda
Kuzman, Colour Washed Canvas,
Donald Southern & Cliff Schorr; 80:
KAT Interiors; 86L: P. Smith & Co.;
86R: Christopher Coleman; 87T:
Michael Lane, artist; 90: Design I, NJ;
103BL: Sandra Morgan Interiors, Inc.;
103R: Jane Irvine, Deerfield, Il; 103TL:
Barry Bishop; 104BR: Anka Pedvisocar,
artist; 105B: Mayflower Inn; 105TL:
Barbara Lazarus, Sue Connell, artist;
105TR: seididesigns.com, artist; 112L:
Anne Olson, architect; 112R: Cathleen
Quandt, architect; 113BR: Phyllis
Grandberg; 113TL: Douglas Wilson;
113TR: Alvaro Ponce; 125B: Christy
Reams, interior decorator; 126R:
Charlotte Moss Interior Design, LLC;
127B: Undercurrent Design; 127T:
paint by Mona Lisa Designs, kitchen
design by Star Norini, Johnson Dis-
tinctive Kitchens, Inc.; 143B: Dianne
Lowenthal Design Group; 144L:
Rachel Samet, ASID, Once Upon A
Design Inc., Winnetka, Il; 145TL: Mel
Crum, ASID, Marshall Fields, Chicago,
Il; 146: Keith Sutherland, architect/
builder; 157B: P. Smith & Co.; 160B:
Jeffrey Lincoln Interiors, Inc.; 160T:
James Coursey; 161BR: Jane Smith,
interior design and Gilda Meyer-
Niehof, stylist; 161TR: Casa Yucatan,
Gibbs Smith Publisher, 2002; 166R:
interior design by Josefina Larrain and
bed design by Paul Fullerton

INDEX

Page numbers in **bold** refer to photograph captions.

A

Acrylics, artist's, 30, **30, 31**
Adhesives, 110, 155
Alcohol, rubbing, 140
Alcoves and arches, 24, **69, 145**
Antique effects
  aged crackle, 55, **164,** 164–165, **165**
  china crackle, 55, **161,** 162, 162–163, **163**
  glaze recipe for, 29
  level of difficulty and key issues, 55
  randomness in, 161, **161**
  weathering or distressed, **161**
Artwork
  artist to paint focal point, **25**
  clouds and sky, 55, **127, 128,** 128–129, **129**
  trompe l'oeil, **12**
  walls which showcase, **10, 27, 57**

B

Baseboard, 45, **45**
Bathrooms, **12, 13, 24, 27, 32, 113, 127**
Birdseed, embedded in plaster, 124, **124**
Borders. *See* Stencils
Brushes
  about, **36,** 36–37
  artist, 39, **39**
  blending, 39, **39**
  chip, **36,** 37, 38–39, **39**
  for decorative effects, 38–40, **39–40**
  flogger, 39, **39**
  how to clean, 50
  linen-effect, 39, **40, 91**
  liner, 141
  stencil, 39, **39**
  stippler, 39, **39**
  strié, 39, **40, 89**
  wallpaper, 40, **40**

C

Ceilings
  "changing" the height of, **7, 10,** 14, **15, 104**
  cloud and sky, **14, 127**
  how to paint, 182, **182**
  masking techniques, 46, **46**
  stencils for, **15, 104, 105**
Chalk lines, 71, 81, **82**
Cheesecloth, 38, **38,** 60–61, **60–61**
Children's rooms, 16, **16–17, 51, 51, 68, 86, 128**
Clean up, 42, 43, 50–51, **50–51,** 114
Cloth, faux
  handwoven, **87**
  linen, 39, **40,** 54, **86, 90,** 90–91, **91**
  silk, 72–74, **72–74**
Color
  black, white, and gray, 20, 22
  choosing (*See* Color selection)
  combined with pattern (*See* Stencils)
  complementary, 20, **21, 23**
  contrast, **8, 27, 56**
  hue, 20
  intensity, 18, 20, **21**
  and light, **18,** 19, **19, 23**
  and mood, 4, 10, 18, **27,** 56
  neutral, 23
  perception of, 19
  primary and secondary, 20, **23**
  temperature, 18
  tertiary and quaternary, 20
  use of two or more, **7, 8, 57,** 116–117, 132–133, **142**
  value, 18
  of wood, 21, **23**
Colorants, 31, **31,** 111, 167, **169,** 180
Color consultant, 21
Color selection
  for dragged effects, 100–101
  for geometric effects, 84–85
  inspiration, **8, 18, 20, 21**
  for metallic effects, 158–159
  for mottled effects, 66–67
  with sample board, 41
  schemes, 18–19, 21–23, 24

Color wheel, 20
Combs, 40, **40, 93, 95**
Contemporary style, **4, 24, 69,** 146, **146**
Corner techniques, 41, **41,** 45, **45,** 46, 70, **117**

D

Doors, **88, 183,** 183–184, **184**
Drop cloths, 42, **42, 134, 179,** 182
Drywall
  primer for, 181
  repair, 174–177, **174–177**
Drywall mud
  application for texture, 34, **34, 35**
  and plaster with mix-ins, 124, **124**
  sanding technique, 179
  to smooth out a textured wall, **178,** 178–179, **179**
  tools for, 40, **178**

F

Feather duster, **52,** 54, 56, 64, **64**
Fiberglass mesh, 174, **175, 177**
Fireplace surrounds, 24
5-in-1 tool, 43, **43**
Float, 125, **125**
Floors
  geometric designs, **14, 15, 17, 68, 105**
  stencils for, **14–15, 17, 104, 105**
Furniture. *See* Projects

G

Gesso, 35, **35**
Gilding, **9,** 55, 142, 154–157, **154–157**
Glaze
  about, 28–29, **29**
  application techniques, 38, 57
  colorwashing with, 28, 56, 58
  metallic, 78
  recipes, 29
Gloves, disposable, 43, 51

H

Holes, how to patch, 174–177, **174–177**

J

Joint compound, 179

L

Laundry area, **25**
Lead, in paint, 185
Leaf, metallic. *See* Gilding
Lighting, **9**, 19, **23**
Lime wash, **10**, 33, 55, 166, 171, 171. *See also* Paints and finishes, lime-base

M

Masking techniques, 44–47, **45, 46,** 50, 71, **71**
Mediterranean style, **7, 9, 12.** *See also* Plaster
Metallic painting techniques
  about, 33
  color selection, 158–159
  faux brushed metal, 55, 146, **146–147,** 147
  faux gold leaf, **136,** 136–137, **137**
  faux hammered metal, 55, **148,** 148–149, **149**
  level of difficulty and key issues, 55
  on pots, 55, 150, **150–153,** 152
  stencil, **6, 33, 143, 144**
  for trim, **9,** 144, **144–145**
Mildew, 185
Molding and trim
  crackle effects, 163
  design painted on, **13**
  faux, **10,** 49, **49, 68, 99**
  glossy paint for, **26**
  metallic, **9,** 144, **144–145, 153**
  pattern design considerations, 88, 90
  as rails or panels, 90, **104**
  in unifying color, 22
Mottling
  about, 54, **56,** 56–57, **57**
  with a brush, 54, 62, **62**
  with cheesecloth, 54, **60,** 60–61, **61**
  color selection, 66–67
  examples, **7, 8, 10–11, 13, 25, 166**
  faux stucco, **8**
  with a feather duster, 52, 54, 64, **64**

level of difficulty and key issues, 54
with a rag, 10, 54, 58, 58–59, 59
by rag rolling, 54, 65, 65
with a two-part roller, 63, 63

N

Newspaper, 134, 135, 141

P

Pad applicators, foam, 37, **37**
Painting surface
  preparation, 27, 42, 44–47, 98, 183
  repairs to, 46, 174–177, **174–177**
  slick, 181, 187
  stains on, 181, 185
  for venetian plaster, 114, 118
Painting techniques
  basic, **48,** 48–49, **49,** 182–187, **182–187**
  colorwashing with glaze, 28, 56, 58
  combed designs, 54, **87,** 92–96, **92–96**
  for corners, 41, **41**
  cutting in, **43,** 48, **48**
  diamonds, **14, 17,** 54, 80–83, **80–83**
  dragged effects, 86–97, **86–97,** 100–101, **143**
  dry-brushed blocks, 54, **78,** 78–79, **79**
  faux antique (*See* Antique effects)
  faux cloth (*See* Cloth, faux)
  faux fresco, **13**
  faux grout or mortar, 68, **68,** 75, **113**
  faux leather, **136,** 136–137, **137**
  faux stone (*See* Stone, faux)
  faux stucco, **8**
  faux suede, 33, **33**
  faux venetian plaster, **9,** 35
  faux wood grain, 39, 55, **88, 127,** 130–131, **130–131**
  frottage, 55, 126, **126, 134,** 134–135, **135**
  grid-based patterns, 93, **93**
  level of difficulty and key issues, 54–55
  metallic effects (*See* Metallic painting techniques)
  mottled effects (*See* Mottling)
  pouncing, 107
  ragging, 38, **38,** 54, 56, 58–61, **58–61**

rag rolling, 54, 65, **65**
rolled squares, 54, **98,** 98–99, **99**
spattering, 55, **132,** 132–133, **133**
stippling, 39, **39**
strié effect, 39, **40,** 54, **88,** 88–89, **89,** 130
stripes (*See* Stripes)
touch-ups, 50, **50,** 98
trial on sample board, 41, 87
writing or lettering, **16, 102**
Paints and finishes
  about, 26–27, 30
  blackboard, 16, 32, **32**
  buying tips, 19
  components, 26
  disposal, 51, **51**
  estimation of amount, 28
  glazes (*See* Glaze)
  glossy, **26,** 183
  glow-in-the-dark, 16, **32,** 32–33
  lime base, **10,** 55, 166, **166, 167,** 168–170, **168–170** (*See also* Lime wash)
  metallic, 33, 78, 142, 150
  mix your own, 30–31
  protective, 29 (*See also* Sealers)
  specialty products, 16, 30–33, 162
  storage, 50–51
  textured, 32, **32, 33,** 34–35, **34–35**
  for trim, **9,** 26, 144, **144–145**
Patterns
  checks, 54, 94–96, **94–96**
  clouds, **14, 127, 128,** 128–129, **129**
  combined with color (*See* Stencils)
  diamonds, **14, 17,** 54, 80–83, **80–83**
  focal-point, **14, 68, 103, 105**
  gameboards, **68**
  grid-based, 93, **93**
  intersection techniques, 68, 70, 80, **83**
  lace designs, 55, 123, **123**
  layout, **70,** 70–71, **71,** 93, **93**
  plaid, **15,** 54, **69,** 97, **97**
  squares, **98,** 98–99, **99**
Pigment, powdered, 30, **30**
Planning
  geometric designs, 70, 79, 81, 84–85

level of difficulty and key issues, 54–55

metal leaf, 157

portability of art panel, **25**

where to use decorative painting, 24, **24–25**

Plaster

crosshatched texture, **23**

faux stone, **113**

level of difficulty and key issues, 55

with mix-ins, 55, **124**, 124–125, **125**

primer for, 181

repair technique, 177, **177**

skip troweling, **112**

tools to apply, 40, **40**

venetian (*See* Venetian plaster)

Polyurethane, 105

Primer

in dry-brushed blocks technique, 78

importance, 27, 172, 180

selection, 181

tinted, 180

Professionals, hiring, 21, **25**

R

Rocker, graining, 39, **39**, 74, **74**

Roller cover, 65, **65**, 99

Roller extension, 37, **182**

Rollers

basic technique, 48–49, **49**

for decorative effects, **11**, 38, **38**, 63, 99

how to clean, 50

painting, 37, **37**, **49**, 184

Rooms

"changing" the size of, 19, **69**, **105**

under eaves, **19**, **105**

S

Safety, 51, 182, 185

Scenes, **12**, **17**

Scrapers and scraping techniques, 43, **43**, 187

Sealers, 105, 125

Shellac, 79

Spackling compound, 174, **174**, 177, **177**

Spatulas, 40, **40**, 114

Sponges, 38, **38**, 56, 76

Squeegee, 40, **40**, 95, **95**, **97**

Stencils

all-over patterns, **6**, **12**, **33**, **104**, **118**, **143**

border, **102**, **103**, **104**, 106–108, **106–108**

brushes for, 39, **39**

for ceilings, **15**, **104**, **105**

diamond, 83

faux molding, **10**, 68

for floors, **14–15**, **17**, **104**, **105**

history, 5

how to secure on wall, 110

level of difficulty and key issues, 55

with lime paint or lime wash, **167**

metallic effects, **6**, **143**

overlay, **103**

pouncing technique, 107

raised, 55, 108–111, **108–111**, **118**

on venetian plaster, **118**, 118–120, **119**, **120**

writing, **16**, **102**

Stone, faux

granite, 132, **132**, **133**

limestone blocks, 54, **68**, 75–77, **75–77**

marble, 39, 55, **127**, 138–141, **138–141**

with plaster, **113**

Straw, embedded in plaster, 55, 125

Stripes

moiré, 54, 72–74, **72–74**

and venetian plaster, **113**

on a wall, **7**, **11**, **17**, 69–74, **69–74**, 98, **142**

T

Tape, masking, 47, **47**, 74. *See also* Masking techniques

Texture

from embedded materials, **124**, 124–125, **125**

embossed, 55, **121**, 121–123, **122**, **123**

frottage, 55, 126, **126**, **134**, 134–135, **135**

from lime wash, 171

paint, 32, **32**, **33**, 34–35, **34–35**

plaster, **23**, **112–113**, 120–123, **120–123**

raised stencils, 108–111, **108–111**

roller covers for, 65, **65**

smoothing out a textured wall, **178**, 178–179, **179**

techniques, 34–35, 38

tissue paper, 55, 136–138, **136–138**

Tools. *See also* Brushes; Rollers

basic accessory equipment, 43, **43**

for clean up, 43, 50, **50**

for decorative effects, 38–40, **38–40**, 93, **93**, 95, **95**, 125

marking, 71

for painting, 36–37, **36–37**

Touch-ups, 50, **50**, 98

Transforming techniques

ceiling height, **7**, **10**, 14, **15**, **104**

mood of a room, 19

size of a room, 19, **69**, **105**

Trim. *See* Molding and trim

Trisodium phosphate (TSP) cleaner, 42, 183, 185, 187

Trompe l'oeil, **12**

Trowels, 40, **40**, 112

V

Vacuum, 179, **186**

Venetian plaster

about, 35, **35**, 55

multicolored, **116**, 116–117, **117**

polished, **7**, **34**, **113**, **114**, 114–115, **115**

stenciled, **118**, 118–120, **119**, **120**

Victorian style, 72, 123

Volatile organic compounds (VOC), 51

W

Wainscot, **142**

Wallpaper, faux. *See* Stencils, all-over patterns

Windows, 185–187, **185–187**

Wood

color, 21, **23**

faux, 39, 55, **88**, **127**, 130–131, **130–131**

primer for, 181

Work area, 179, 182

Writing or lettering, **16**, **102**